New Frontiers in Regional Science: Asian Perspectives

Volume 22

New Frontiers in Regional Science: Asian Perspectives

This series is a constellation of works by scholars in the field of regional science and in related disciplines specifically focusing on dynamism in Asia.

Asia is the most dynamic part of the world. Japan, Korea, Taiwan, and Singapore experienced rapid and miracle economic growth in the 1970s. Malaysia, Indonesia, and Thailand followed in the 1980s. China, India, and Vietnam are now rising countries in Asia and are even leading the world economy. Due to their rapid economic development and growth, Asian countries continue to face a variety of urgent issues including regional and institutional unbalanced growth, environmental problems, poverty amidst prosperity, an ageing society, the collapse of the bubble economy, and deflation, among others.

Asian countries are diversified as they have their own cultural, historical, and geographical as well as political conditions. Due to this fact, scholars specializing in regional science as an inter- and multi-discipline have taken leading roles in providing mitigating policy proposals based on robust interdisciplinary analysis of multifaceted regional issues and subjects in Asia. This series not only will present unique research results from Asia that are unfamiliar in other parts of the world because of language barriers, but also will publish advanced research results from those regions that have focused on regional and urban issues in Asia from different perspectives.

The series aims to expand the frontiers of regional science through diffusion of intrinsically developed and advanced modern regional science methodologies in Asia and other areas of the world. Readers will be inspired to realize that regional and urban issues in the world are so vast that their established methodologies still have space for development and refinement, and to understand the importance of the interdisciplinary and multidisciplinary approach that is inherent in regional science for analyzing and resolving urgent regional and urban issues in Asia.

Topics under consideration in this series include the theory of social cost and benefit analysis and criteria of public investments, socio-economic vulnerability against disasters, food security and policy, agro-food systems in China, industrial clustering in Asia, comprehensive management of water environment and resources in a river basin, the international trade bloc and food security, migration and labor market in Asia, land policy and local property tax, Information and Communication Technology planning, consumer "shop-around" movements, and regeneration of downtowns, among others.

More information about this series at http://www.springer.com/series/13039

Melba Falck-Reyes • Leo Guzman-Anaya
Editors

Japanese Direct Investment in Mexico's Transport Equipment Sector

Macro Impact and Local Responses

Springer

Editors
Melba Falck-Reyes
Pacific Studies Department
University of Guadalajara
Zapopan, Mexico

Leo Guzman-Anaya
Human Resources Department
University of Guadalajara
Zapopan, Mexico

ISSN 2199-5974 ISSN 2199-5982 (electronic)
New Frontiers in Regional Science: Asian Perspectives
ISBN 978-981-10-7717-3 ISBN 978-981-10-7718-0 (eBook)
https://doi.org/10.1007/978-981-10-7718-0

Library of Congress Control Number: 2017963130

Printed on acid-free paper

This Springer imprint is published by the registered company Springer Nature Singapore Pte Ltd.
The registered company address is: 152 Beach Road, #21-01/04 Gateway East, Singapore 189721, Singapore

Preface

Presently the global chains of production organize their activities in such a way that foreign direct investment (FDI) by multinational companies (MNCs) has important effects on the host country, not only at the macroeconomic level as in trade but also on the competitiveness of the localities that are the direct beneficiaries of those flows of investment. Furthermore, the fragmentation of production carried out by MNCs opens new opportunities to local suppliers to engage in such chains of production and also benefit from training programs to enhance productivity.

In the past decades, Mexico has been favored by important flows of investment with Japan as the major investor from Asia and the second foreign investor in the Mexican transport equipment sector. Notwithstanding, there has been a shortage of academic comprehensive research on the effects of the Japan FDI. Thus, motivated by this state of affairs, in 2015, the authors of the chapters in this volume, who had previous experience on Japanese studies as researchers at the University of Guadalajara in Mexico, took the initiative to carry out a comprehensive study to evaluate the impact of JFDI in Mexico through a multidisciplinary approach to contribute to fill the gap. The purpose of the project was to assess the impact and the dynamics of JFDI both at the macro and local levels, concentrating on the formation of production networks in the North American region, on the role of fostering a regional cluster on the central states of Mexico (the Bajío region), and on the impact on local entities in developing local suppliers, training human resources, and transferring technology.

We would like to express our gratitude to the University of Guadalajara, especially to the Pacific Studies Department of the University Center for Social Sciences and Humanities and to the Human Resources Department, and Mexico-Japan Studies Program of the University Center for Economic and Administrative Sciences for providing a research environment to carry out this project. We also thank the National Council for Science and Technology of Mexico for the support given to one of the members of the group under the auspices of the program of repatriation of Mexican academics. We extend a special appreciation and recognition to Professor Yoshiro Higano from Springer for believing in this project and for all his valuable comments that improved our manuscript. We also thank the support of the team of editors from Springer. Needless to say, the usual disclaimer applies. Melba Falck-Reyes would like to thank Esteban Alcalá López and Ligia Ibarra González for their research assistance. We believe that the topics dealt with in the book can be of special interest to Asia-Pacific readers, since they cover a well-established trans-pacific integration between Japan and Mexico.

Melba Falck-Reyes
Leo Guzman-Anaya

Contents

1 **Introduction: Relevance of the Transport Equipment Sector in Mexico** 1
Melba Falck-Reyes and Leo Guzman-Anaya

2 **Japanese Foreign Direct Investment in Mexico's Transport Equipment Sector. The Macro Impact: Regional Networks of Production and Trade** 9
Melba Falck-Reyes

3 **Locational Determinants of Japanese Automotive FDI in Mexico: A Spatial Analysis** 31
Leo Guzman-Anaya

4 **Spillovers of Japanese Automotive Companies' Activities in the State of Aguascalientes** 55
Emma Mendoza Martínez

5 **The Role of Public Policies in Attracting Japanese FDI in Mexico** 81
Maria Guadalupe Lugo-Sanchez

6 **The Impact of Japanese Training Programs on Local Automotive Suppliers' Productivity in Mexico's State of Guanajuato** 103
Leo Guzman-Anaya

Abbreviations

AAEMJ	Mexico-Japan Economic Partnership Agreement (Acuerdo de Asociación Económica México-Japón)
ACT	Multinational Accompaniment Model
ALADI	Latin American Association of Integration (Asociación Latinoamericana de Integración)
AMDA	Mexican Association of Automobiles Distributors (Asociación Mexicana de Distribuidores de Automotores)
AMEXCID	Mexican Agency of International Cooperation for Development (Agencia Mexicana de Cooperación Internacional para el Desarrollo)
AMIA	Mexican Association of the Automotive Industry (Asociación Mexicana de la Industria Automotriz)
ANPACT	National Association of Production of Auto Parts and Trucks (Asociación Nacional de Producción de Autopartes, Camiones y Tractocamiones)
ANPQP	Alliance New Product Quality Procedure
APEC	Asia-Pacific Economic Cooperation Council
ASEAN	Association of South East Asian Nations
CAR	Center for Automotive Research
CASCI	Collaboration Activities with Suppliers for Continuous Improvement, Mexico
CECOI	Center for Competitiveness and Innovation Mexico (Centro de Competitividad e Innovación, México)
CeDIAM	Center for Development of the Automotive Industry in Mexico (Centro de Desarrollo de la Industria Automotriz en México)
CEOs	Chief Executive Officers
CIATEQ	Center for Advanced Technology, Mexico (Centro de Tecnología Avanzada, México)
CIMAT	Mathematical Research Center, Aguascalientes, Mexico (Centro de Investigación en Matemáticas, Aguascalientes, México)

CIO	Center for Optic Research, Aguascalientes, Mexico (Centro de Investigación Óptica, Aguascalientes, México)
CITTAA	Aguascalientes Center for Innovation and Technology Transfer for the Automotive Sector, Mexico (Centro de Innovación y Transferencia Tecnológica de Aguascalientes Aguascalientes, México)
CLIAB	Logistic Corridor of the Bajio Automotive Industry (Corredor Logístico Industrial Automotriz del Bajío)
COMPITE	National Committee of Productivity and Innovation (Comité Nacional de Productividad e Innovación Tecnológica)
CONACyT	National Council of Science and Technology (Consejo Nacional de Ciencia y Tecnología)
CONALEP	National College of Technical Professional Education, Mexico (Colegio Nacional de Educación Profesional Técnica, México)
CONEVAL	National Council of Social Development Policy Evaluation (Consejo Nacional de Evaluación de la Política de Desarrollo Social)
EPA	Mexico-Japan Economic Partnership Agreement
EYGM	Ernst & Young Global Limited
FDI	Foreign Direct Investment
FE	Fixed Effects
FTAs	Free Trade Agreements
GDP	Gross Domestic Product
GIRAA	Industry Group of the Automotive Branch of Aguascalientes, Mexico (Grupo de Industrias del Ramo Automotriz de Aguascalientes, México)
GIS	Geographic Information System
GVC	Global Value Chains
ICT	Information, Communications and Technology
IDB	Inter-American Development Bank
IDEPMEX	Institute for Suppliers Development, Mexico (Instituto para el Desarrollo de Proveedores de México)
IECA	Training State Institute (Instituto Estatal de Capacitación)
INA	National Industry of Auto Parts (Industria Nacional de Autopartes, A.C.)
INADEM	National Institute of the Entrepreneur (Instituto Nacional del Emprendedor)
INEGI	National Institute of Statistics and Geography (Instituto Nacional de Estadística y Geografía)
ISN	Tax on Payroll (Impuesto Sobre Nómina)
IT	Information Technology
ITA	Aguascalientes Institute of Technology, Mexico (Instituto Tecnológico de Aguascalientes, México)
ITESM	Monterrey Institute of Technology and Higher Education (Instituto Tecnológico de Estudios Superiores de Monterrey)

JBIC	Japan Bank for International Cooperation
JCC	Joint Coordination Committee
JETRO	Japan External Trade Organization
JFDI	Japanese Foreign Direct Investment
JICA	Japan International Cooperation Agency
JMEPA	Japan-Mexico Economic Partnership Agreement
JPCS	Japanese Production Control Systems
LISA	Local Indicator of Spatial Association
MDD	Millions of Dollars
MERCOSUR	Southern Common Market (Mercado Común del Cono Sur)
METI	Ministry of Economy, Trade and Industry
MNs	Multinational firms
MSMEs	Micro, Small and Medium Size Enterprises
NAFTA	North American Free Trade Agreement
NHTS	National Highway Traffic Safety, US Department of Transportation
NIES	New Industrialized Countries
ODA	Official Development Assistance
OECD	Organisation for Economic Co-operation and Development
OEMs	Original Equipment Manufacturers
OICA	International Organization of Motor Vehicles Manufacturers
OLS	Ordinary Least Squares
PASCDM	Project for Automotive Supply Chain Development in Mexico
PDM	Project Design Matrix
PEI	Innovation Stimulus Program, Mexico (Programa de Estímulos a la Innovación, México)
PSC	Process Statistical Control
QCD	Quality, Costs and Delivery
R&D	Research and Development
RE	Random Effects
RIETI	Research Institute of Economy, Trade and Industry, Japan
RIPPAS	Reciprocal Investment Promotion and Protection Agreements
SAR	Spatial Auto-Regressive
SCI	State Competitiveness Index
SD	Spatial Durbin
SE	Secretariat of Economy (Secretaría de Economía)
SEDEC	Secretary for Economic Development, Aguascalientes, Mexico (Secretaría de Desarrollo Económico, Aguascalientes, México)
SEM	Spatial Error Model
SEZ	Special Economic Zones
SMEs	Small and Medium Size Enterprises
SQC	Statistical Quality Control
TE	Transport Equipment Sector
TPs	Training Programs
U.K.	United Kingdom
U.S.	United States

UAA	Autonomous University of Aguascalientes, Mexico (Universidad Autónoma de Aguascalientes, México)
UNCTAD	United Nations Conference on Trade and Development
UNDP	United Nations Development Program
UPA	Polytechnic University of Aguascalientes, Mexico (Universidad Politécnica de Aguascalientes, México)
USA	United States of America
USD	United States Dollars
WTO	World Trade Organization

List of Figures

Fig. 1.1 Total Japanese FDI flows to Mexico in million constant 2010 U.S. Dollars. 1996–2015 (Source: Authors' calculations with information from JETRO (2017), SE (2017) and OECD (2017)) 4

Fig. 2.1 Mexico and Japan: evolution of exports and imports. 1995–2015 Thousands of US dollars Source: Own elaboration with information of Mexico's Ministry of Economy for data related to imports and JETRO-Mexico with information from the Ministry of Finance of Japan, for data related to exports to Japan http://www.economia-snci.gob.mx/ https://www.jetro.go.jp/mexico/ 13

Fig. 2.2 Mexico: evolution of trade balance by main regions. 1995–2015 Thousands of US dollars Source: Own elaboration with information from RIETI-TID 2015 and Mexico's Ministry of Economy http://www.rieti-tid.com/trade.php http://www.gob.mx/se/ 14

Fig. 2.3 Mexico: flows of FDI and projects announced by Japanese companies. 2003–2016 Flows of investment in Millions of US dollars Number of projects on top of each column Source: Own elaboration with information from The Financial Times (2017) fDiMarkets.com Trends Report: FDI from Japan to Mexico. January 2003 to June 2017 15

Map 2.1 Location of Japanese affiliates in Mexico. 2015 Numbers represent the Japanese affiliates operating in the selected states Source: Own elaboration with information of the Secretariat of Economy Mexico and JETRO-Mexico. http://www.gob.mx/se/ https://www.jetro.go.jp/mexico/ 16

Fig. 2.4 Mexico: evolution of employment in the transport equipment sector. 2007–2016 Number of jobs by main

	category Source: Own elaboration with information of INEGI Mexico www.inegi.org.mx	17
Diagram 2.1	Japanese affiliates operating in Asia and North America and flows of intermediate goods 2015 Source: Own elaboration with information from RIETI-TID 2015 and the Summary of the 46th Survey on Overseas Business Activities, 2016 http://www.rieti-tid.com/trade.php http://www.meti.go.jp/english/statistics/tyo/kaigaizi/index.html Note: *ASEAN* Association of South East Asian Nations, *NIES* New Industrialized Countries	19
Fig. 2.5	Mexico: evolution of imports of intermediate goods. Share by main regions. 1995–2015 Percentages (%) Source: Own elaboration with information from RIETI-TID 2015. http://www.rieti-tid.com/trade.php	20
Fig. 2.6	Mexico: evolution of imports of intermediate goods in the transport equipment sector. Share by main regions. 1995–2015 Percentages (%) Source: Own elaboration with information from RIETI-TID 2015. http://www.rieti-tid.com/trade.php	22
Fig. 2.7	Japanese brands of motor vehicles sold in the US market by final assembly country. Local, regional and foreign procurement ratios. 2016 Percentages (%) Source: Own elaboration with data from NHTSA, U.S. Department of Transportation, National Highway Traffic Safety Administration. http://www.nhtsa.gov/	23
Fig. 2.8	Mexico: evolution of exports of final goods in transport equipment sector by main regions. 1995–2015 Thousands of US dollars Source: Own elaboration with information from RIETI-2015 http://www.rieti-tid.com/trade.php	24
Fig. 2.9	Mexico: evolution of exports of intermediate goods in transport equipment sector by main regions. 1995–2015 Thousands of US dollars Source: Own elaboration with information from RIETI-TID 2015. http://www.rieti-tid.com/trade.php	24
Fig. 2.10	Mexico: evolution of trade balance in the transportation equipment sector. 1995–2015 Thousands of US dollars Source: Own elaboration with information from RIETI-TID 2015. http://www.rieti-tid.com/trade.php	25
Fig. 3.1	The distribution of Japanese automotive supplier firms across Mexican municipalities, 2015 (Source: Author's calculations based on data from Toyo Keizai (2015/2016))	33
Fig. 3.2	The distribution of Japanese automotive assemblers and suppliers in Mexico, 2015 (Source: Author's calculations based on data from Toyo Keizai (2015/2016))	34

Fig. 3.3 LISA Cluster map 2000 (Source: Author's calculations based on data from Toyo Keizai (2015/2016)) 47
Fig. 3.4 LISA Cluster map 2005 (Source: Author's calculations based on data from Toyo Keizai (2015/2016)) 48
Fig. 3.5 LISA Cluster map 2010 (Source: Author's calculations based on data from Toyo Keizai (2015/2016)) 48

Fig. 5.1 FDI flows to Mexico, in current prices and millions of USD (1980–2015) Source: Author's own elaboration with data from UNCTAD 82
Fig. 5.2 FDI flows to Mexico as GDP percentage (1980–2015) Source: Author's own elaboration with data from UNCTAD ... 83
Fig. 5.3 Total Japanese FDI flows, outward – millions of USD (1980–2015) Source: Author's own elaboration with data from UNCTAD 83
Fig. 5.4 FDI distribution by sectors in Mexico, 2016. In percentages Source: Author's own elaboration with data from SE 87
Fig. 5.5 FDI distribution in Mexico's automotive sector, 2016. In percentages Source: Author's own elaboration with data from SE 88
Fig. 5.6 FDI flows to Mexico's automotive sector by country of origin, 2016. In millions of USD Source: Author's own elaboration with data from SE 89
Fig. 5.7 Percentage of total FDI vs Japanese FDI flows to Mexico, (1999–2016) Source: Author's own elaboration with data from SE 89
Fig. 5.8 Japanese FDI received by state, in millions of USD (1999–2016) Source: Author's own elaboration with data from SE 90
Fig. 5.9 Number of fiscal incentives for FDI attraction offered by state and municipality, 2015 Source: Author's own elaboration with data from State Governments and/or State Secretariats of Economic Development, 2015 91
Fig. 5.10 National growth rate, compared to Bajio states growth rate. 2004–2015. In percentages Source: Author's own elaboration with data from INEGI 97
Fig. 5.11 National manufacturing sector growth rate, compared to Bajio states growth rate. 2004–2015. In percentages Source: Author's own elaboration with data from INEGI 98
Fig. 5.12 Unemployment rate for Bajio states. 2004–2015. In percentages Source: Author's own elaboration with data from INEGI 98

Fig. 6.1 JICA Training Participants from Mexico 1958–2013 (Source: Author's calculations based on data from JICA 2016) 104

Fig. 6.2 Total Automobile Production in Mexico 2014–2016 (Source: Author's calculations based on data from AMIA 2016)........ 108
Fig. 6.3 Flow diagram of PASCDM for Guanajuato State (Source: Author's elaboration using data from JICA 2015)........ 119
Fig. 6.4 Action plan diagram of PASCDM for Guanajuato State (Source: Author's elaboration using data from JICA 2015)........ 120

List of Tables

Table 3.1	Tobit model estimation results	44
Table 3.2	Negative binomial model estimation results	46
Table 3.3	Moran's I statistic for spatial autocorrelation, 2000, 2005 and 2010	47
Table 3.4	SAR and SD model estimation results	49
Table 4.1	Support programs to SMEs of Aguascalientes, suppliers of the automotive sector	64
Table 5.1	Fiscal incentives for FDI attraction per state and municipalities in Mexico, 2015	92
Table 5.2	Fiscal incentives by state in the Bajio Region	93
Table 5.3	Ranking of the Bajio states per competitiveness index	96
Table 6.1	Automotive supplier structure in Mexico (2010)	110
Table 6.2	Training courses offered for government officials and tier-2 firms during the PASCDM	112
Table 6.3	Overall objective and results from the PASCDM	113
Table 6.4	Results from the superior objective	114
Table 6.5	Results from the expected result #1	115
Table 6.6	Results from the expected result #2	115
Table 6.7	Results from the expected result #3	116
Table 6.8	Results from the expected result #4	117
Table 6.9	Results from the expected result #5	118
Table 6.10	Phase 1 technical assistance plan and results for Guanajuato State (Six firms)	121
Table 6.11	Phase 2 technical assistance plan and results for Guanajuato State (Nine firms)	123
Table 6.12	Detailed results from phase 1 for Guanajuato State (Six firms)	129
Table 6.13	Detailed results from phase 2 for Guanajuato State (Nine firms)	130

Chapter 1
Introduction: Relevance of the Transport Equipment Sector in Mexico

Melba Falck-Reyes and Leo Guzman-Anaya

Abstract Currently, Mexico stands out in the automotive industry as one of the major producers and exporters of the world. The country has become an attractive destination for foreign direct investment that take advantage of favorable economic and political environment and the formation of "near shore" production networks in North America. As a source of investment, Japan has become the second major investor in the Mexican automotive industry. This chapter provides an overview of the importance and structure of the automotive industry in the Mexican economy and the role that Japanese foreign direct investment is playing in the Mexican Transport Equipment sector lead by Japanese Multinationals and their network of suppliers. The final section of this introductory chapter summarizes the content of the book.

Keywords Automotive and autoparts industry · Japanese Foreign Direct Investment · Networks of production

1.1 The Transport Equipment Sector in Mexico

Total global light vehicle and heavy vehicle production was registered in 2015 at 86.9 million and 3.7 million units respectively. From this, Mexico produced 3.4 million of light vehicles and exported 2.8 million units making it the 7th overall producer and 4th exporter worldwide. For heavy vehicles, production and exports were registered at 191,000 and 156,900 units respectively, achieving the 5th overall producer and 4th overall exporter positions (Promexico 2016).

M. Falck-Reyes (✉)
Pacific Studies Department, University of Guadalajara, Zapopan, Mexico
e-mail: mefalck@gmail.com

L. Guzman-Anaya
Human Resources Department, University of Guadalajara, Zapopan, Mexico
e-mail: leo.guzman8@gmail.com

M. Falck-Reyes, L. Guzman-Anaya (eds.), *Japanese Direct Investment in Mexico's Transport Equipment Sector*, New Frontiers in Regional Science: Asian Perspectives 22,
https://doi.org/10.1007/978-981-10-7718-0_1

Restrictions on automotive FDI were reduced dramatically with the implementation of NAFTA in 1994 and were further reduced in 2000 by eliminating the national content requirement to FDI on new vehicles and easing location restrictions within major Mexican cities (Lichtensztejn 2014). Also, after the 2008 financial crisis, Mexico consolidated its position as an attractive manufacturing destination as firms shifted from cost-optimization strategies and searched for closer suppliers that could provide immediate inputs especially for the North American automotive market. This shift in production continued to move plants from American, European and Asian Original Equipment Manufacturers (OEMs) to Mexico to take advantage of quality manufacturing with a cost-competitive element and the preferential benefits of the North American Free Trade Agreement (NAFTA) and Mexico's other 11 Free Trade Agreements (FTAs) that provide access to forty-six countries and over 60% of world GDP (Global Business Reports 2016). Thus, from the total automotive production in Mexico, 80% is exported to more than 100 countries with 73% concentrated in the United States and Canada.

The automotive and auto parts industries have proven to be key areas for the Mexican economy. According to data from Promexico (2016), in 2015 these industries represented 3% of Mexico's GDP, 18% of manufacturing GDP, 27% of total exports and employed over 875,000 workers. Also, in terms of Foreign Direct Investment (FDI), automotive firms accounted for 20% of total investment received in Mexico in 2015. In particular, from the total FDI in the transport industry, 46% was to the terminal automotive industry and 54% to the auto parts industry (including tires). It is estimated by CAR (2017) that 65% of total FDI in Mexico across all industries is automotive supplier related and suppliers are mainly from the U.S. (19%), Japan (18%) and Germany (12%) with most of them having operations across North America.

The development of the automotive and auto parts industries has created production hubs in the center and northern part of Mexico. In total, 14 out of the 32 Mexican states have vehicle production.[1] This contributed to a geographical redistribution of economic activity from an agglomeration in Mexico City to the emergence of regional production hubs in the northern and center of the country. The geographical distribution of the Mexican automotive industry creates a supply chain that can easily adapt to market changing demand and natural disasters that provide competitive production costs and low supply chain risk. Also, NAFTA has created an interconnected supply chain in the United States, Canada and Mexico, supported by domestic and "near shore" production that supports employment within the region. The production of automotive parts and components in Mexico rather than "off-shore" helped develop and sustain a competitive automotive industry across North America that might have otherwise relocated to lower-wage countries in Asia, Eastern Europe or South America (CAR 2017).

Currently, the automotive industry of Mexico has at the top 20 Original Equipment Manufacturers (OEM) that assemble the final brand products, mainly

[1] These states include: Aguascalientes, Baja California, Chihuahua, Coahuila, Guanajuato, Hidalgo, Jalisco, Estado de Mexico, Morelos, Nuevo Leon, Puebla, Queretaro, San Luis Potosi and Sonora.

companies from North America, Germany and Japan. Among the Japanese ones stand out Toyota, Nissan, Mazda, Honda, Mitsubishi, Suzuki and Subaru (Fuji Heavy Industries). In the supply chain, the Tier 1 suppliers work directly with the OEMs, supplying complex components and collaborating jointly in design. There are about 350 Tier 1 suppliers in Mexico, all of them foreign Multinationals, which supply to different OEMs (APEC 2017). Downstream the supply chain, Tier 2 suppliers produce value adding parts and components that are delivered to Tier 1 suppliers.[2] There are about 400 companies at this level of supply in Mexico, but just 30% of them are Mexican. According to EYGM (2017) Tier 2 Mexican companies' have a low share in the market for stamping, foundry, forging and machining, that range from 25% to 35%. Finally, the Tier 3 level suppliers provide simpler engineered materials and services to Tier 2 suppliers. There are about 2290 auto parts Mexican suppliers at this level.[3]

If we add to the above system of producers, the companies in charge of sales, distribution and post-sales services, we have the whole picture for the automotive sector. There are 1972 distribution agencies in Mexico.[4] From the above description of the Mexican automotive industry, is clear that one of the main challenges for Mexico, as a host country of important foreign flows of investment is how to incorporate more Small and Medium Enterprises in the automotive supply chain.[5]

1.2 Japanese Foreign Direct Investment in Mexico: The Transport Equipment Sector

As a result of the Plaza accord of 1985, Japanese Foreign Direct Investment (JFDI) increased worldwide, primarily to Asia and the United States, since Japanese products were losing competitiveness in international markets as result of the appreciation of the Japanese Yen.

For the case of JFDI in Mexico, investment has grown significantly after the implementation of the Mexico-Japan Economic Partnership Agreement (EPA) in 2005 and this growth has been more accentuated since 2012. Figure 1.1 depicts official JFDI statistics to Mexico from the Japan External Organization (JETRO 2017a), the Organisation for Economic Co-operation and Development (OECD 2017) and Mexico's Secretariat of Economy (SE 2017). The graph shows an important increase of JFDI flows after 2011, which corresponds to the arrival of Japanese automotive assemblers and suppliers primarily to the western region of Mexico.

[2] In some specific cases Tier 2 suppliers may also supply OEM's directly.

[3] Figures for Mexican companies at each level of the supply chain came from APEC (2017).

[4] See Chap. 2 by Melba Falck-Reyes for a detailed analysis of employment in the automotive sector.

[5] See Chaps. 3 by Leo Guzman-Anaya and Chap. 4 by Emma Mendoza Martínez for particular discussions regarding Japanese cooperation in these matters.

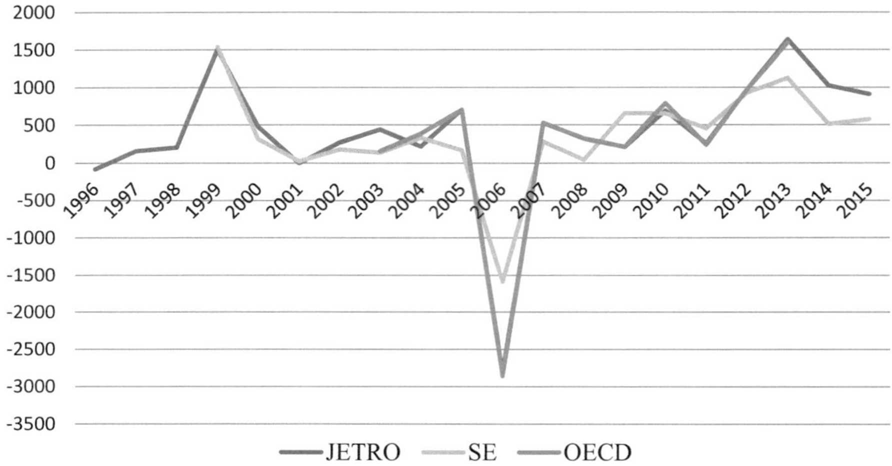

Fig. 1.1 Total Japanese FDI flows to Mexico in million constant 2010 U.S. Dollars. 1996–2015 (**Source:** Authors' calculations with information from JETRO (2017), SE (2017) and OECD (2017))

Salas (2016) mentions that the total number of Japanese companies grew from 399 in 2009 to 1111 in 2016 and the total number of Japanese nationals residing in Mexico went from 6046 in 2008 to 9437 in 2015. According to the "Quarterly Survey of Overseas Subsidiaries" from Japan's Ministry of Economy, Trade and Industry (METI 2017), there has been an important growth in sales and number of employees in Japanese subsidiaries established in Mexico. By comparing quarters in 2015 and 2016, sales have grown from 5% to 15% and employment from 7% to 12%, reflecting a favorable environment for business activities from Japanese multinationals. Also, according to the Japan Bank for International Cooperation, the country moved from the 12th position in 2011 to the 6th in 2015 in terms of Japanese FDI attraction index, an index that ranks countries in terms of promising regions for business development over the medium term (3 years or so) (JBIC 2016).

Historically, JFDI has been concentrated in the manufacturing sector. According to data from Mexico's Secretariat of Economy (SE 2017), between 1999 and 2016, over 82% of total JFDI concentrated in manufacturing activities. From the manufacturing industry, the transport equipment sector stands out accounting for over 57% of total JFDI between 1999 and 2016, followed by the manufacturing of electronic components and computer equipment with less than 8%. Turning to the transport equipment sector, in 2016 Japanese automotive assemblers accounted a little over 40% of total automobile production and total exports in the industry. The boom of JFDI flows in general and the increasing interest of investment in the transport equipment sector is followed by two main factors: The strategic location of Mexico as a production base for exports to the North American (U.S. and Canada) and South American market (mainly Brazil), and by an increasing internal demand for automotive products. Other factors that have contributed to the arrival of automotive firms in Mexico, according to Promexico (2016), include the presence of infrastructure, competitive costs and a highly qualified labor force. Also, Salas (2016) argues that from the point of view of Japanese firms, a solid political system, stable economic and fiscal policies and favorable labor conditions are seen as competitive advantages for investing in Mexico. These achievements have positioned the country as the overall seventh producer and fourth exporter of light vehicles worldwide. It is important to point out that Japanese multinational assembly plants that have moved production from their home regions to Mexico will increasingly rely on the presence of supply chains in North America, given the logistical disadvantage from overseas sourcing of parts and components (CAR 2017).

Despite the clear renewed interest in Mexico's automotive industry, there are still clear challenges ahead. One question that remains is: what does all this industry development mean for the local firms and its human capital? It has been seen that OEMs bring their own supplier network limiting the opportunities and crowding out possible new local suppliers. In an industry characterized by trust and long-term relationships it becomes relevant for local players to become cost competitive and apt in terms of quality as their foreign counterparts. Another challenge for local firms is the transition to innovation and design activities within Mexico. As the Global Business Reports (2016) points out, R&D public investment in Mexico is only 0.6% of GDP, while similar economies invest over 4% of GDP. Access to finance is another entry barrier for local firms. Mexican firms find it difficult and costly to access the availability of credit in comparison to foreign firms affecting negatively their development. Local governments may play an important role taking concrete actions to provide financial support and support their development. The main opportunities for local players lie in the Tier-1 and Tier-2 levels of procurement, where more than half of needed inputs are still imported.

For the case of human capital, the industry has worked with academic institutions to ensure the supply of technicians and engineers given the increasing demand for skilled labor. However, in many cases this has not been enough, with several geographic automotive areas experiencing labor shortages and universities and technical centers failing to catch up to a constantly evolving industry. The short-term challenge is bestowed on the need to offer human capital development programs within the firms to reduce high labor turnover rates and for Universities to offer more specialized training with hands on experience according to the industry's specific needs. In the long-term, the future for human capital seems to be within R&D and innovation. Almost 12,000 engineers graduate each year from various public and private institutions and the setting up of engineering and design centers seems like the next step for human development in Mexico (Global Business Reports 2016). It becomes relevant to continue to build synergies between the three levels of government (federal, state and municipal), the private sector (foreign and local automotive firms) and private and public educational institutions to increase business competitiveness in the industry.

The recent victory of the Republican Party's presidential candidate Donald Trump in November 2016 and a possible change of direction towards a more protectionist trade policy for the U.S. threaten global economic integration processes and multilateralism as mechanisms to reduce poverty and stimulate economic growth (Granados 2016). For the case of the automotive industry, major changes in the tariff structure could hamper automotive manufacturers in delivering affordable vehicles according to consumer demand and may break a regionally integrated and complex web of supplier relations reducing the ability from the supply chain to meet globally competitive requirements in terms of costs and quality. Given this scenario, it becomes relevant for the Mexican public and private sectors to strengthen the internal economy and diversify trade relations with other parts of the world, where the Latin America and Asia Pacific region represent a growing and dynamic prospect for trade and investment opportunities for Mexico. According to Tadashi Minemura, General Director in Mexico of the Japan External Trade Organization (JETRO), despite this upcoming period of uncertainty in the U.S. market, Japanese automotive firms in Mexico "cannot forget the United States, but they can also look to Europe and South America" (Magaña 2016:28).

1.3 Purpose and Structure of the Book

The purpose of this book is to present a variety of empirical research on Japanese FDI taking the highly relevant case of the transport equipment sector within the Mexican context. It has been argued that the increase of Japanese FDI flows to Mexico were incentivized by factors such as the network of Free Trade Agreements (FTAs) signed by Mexico, the growing internal and neighboring markets as well as by the presence of an established supplier base and skilled workforce for the Transport Equipment sector in particular. Also, state and local governments have responded with public policies that facilitate investment flows seeking to attract Japanese firms to their entities and benefit from the spillover effects associated with FDI. From newly constituted databases, the regional distribution of Japanese firms seems to follow a spatial agglomeration of production that might be fostering production hubs in the central, western and northern parts of Mexico. The aim of the book consists in presenting macro-level impacts and micro-level responses to obtain new evidence on the effects associated to Japanese FDI in a developing country.

Following the introductory chapter, the book consists of five chapters. In Chap. 2 Melba Falck-Reyes introduces the role of Japanese automotive firms established in Mexico in creating regional networks of production and trade. With arrival of Japanese firms through production networks, impacts are expected at the macro level in terms of intra and inter-regional trade flows of intermediate and final goods increasing economic integration through multinational firms (MNs). The analysis is based on the fragmentation of production theory and focuses on how the flow of imports and exports of intermediate and final goods from Japanese MNs have impacted the intra- and inter-regional trade flows and economic integration for Mexico. The results are more noticeable for the NAFTA region, however an important rise in trade with the Asian region is indicative of the importance from Japanese firms in the increase in production and employment of the automotive industry. In this sense, Japanese MNs seem to play an important role in fostering production networks within the NAFTA region and Asia primarily.

In Chap. 3 Leo Guzman-Anaya presents an analysis on the regional location determinants of Japanese automotive firms in Mexico. It is argued that foreign firms benefit from spatially agglomerated industries and also that Japanese firms are influenced by factors related to regional demand, regional production costs, regional infrastructure, policy incentives, and existence of agglomerated industries, mainly with presence of other Japanese firms. Using spatial econometric tools and municipal data it is shown that Japanese firms exhibit a preference for agglomeration in production location that eases the transition to the Mexican context and favors the development of the supply chain that allows integration with future customers and suppliers.

Emma Mendoza focuses on the demonstration effect from Japanese firms located within Aguascalientes in Chap. 4. The case of Aguascalientes stands out with the arrival of Nissan in 1959 as an automotive distributor and later in 1982 establishing an assembly plant in the state. The long presence of Nissan and its extensive network of Tier-1 suppliers along with the cooperation with local governments, research centers and Universities and the benefits to the local economy are examined through the demonstration effect framework. Specifically, the analysis seeks to find demonstration spillovers through the development of local suppliers and their later integration into Japanese companies' production chains. In this sense, progress is shown but challenges lay ahead, especially for the case of Small and Medium Size Enterprises (SMEs), whom exhibit intrinsic limitations that prevent them from integrating into Japanese production networks.

The aim of Chap. 5 by Maria Guadalupe Lugo-Sanchez is to analyze the role of public polices from state governments in attracting Japanese automotive firms. Local governments seek to benefit from the presence of FDI in their entities and fiscal policies stand out as mechanisms to attract these firms. Japanese firms seem responsive to fiscal incentives related to exemptions or reductions on acquisitions of real estate for new projects and employment benefits. However, other factors related to regional demand, regional production costs, regional infrastructure, and existence of agglomeration also influence the location of Japanese automotive firms in Mexico.

In Chap. 6 Leo Guzman-Anaya discusses the role of Training Programs (TPs) as mechanisms for technological and knowledge transfer to local firms and the productivity gains from these programs. The increasing presence of new Original Equipment Manufacturers (OEMs) and Tier-1 suppliers from Japan has also influenced the gradual development of networks of local suppliers and augmented demand and training of human resources at the local level. This in turn, has set pressure for federal, state and local governments, especially in the Bajío Region, to respond by cooperating with Japanese companies and Japanese development agencies to set in motion training programs for local suppliers, mainly at the Tier-2 level of procurement. The analysis is focused on the "Project for Automotive Supply Chain Development in Mexico" that was promoted between Japanese and Mexican development agencies together with state governments of Guanajuato, Queretaro and Nuevo Leon. Overall positive results are found from the project showing local firms learn and implement Japanese style production methods that impact their productivity; however, limitations from Mexican SMEs also are exhibited diminishing the benefits from the TPs.

References

APEC Policy Support Unit. (2017, May). *Supporting industry promotion policies in APEC- case study on Mexico*. APEC Policy Support Unit, APEC Publications. http://publications.apec.org/file-download.php?filename=217_PSU_Final%20Report_Case%20Study%20on%20Supporting%20Industry_Mexico.pdf&id=1863. Accessed 30 June 2017.

CAR. (2017). *NAFTA briefing: Trade benefits to the automotive industry and potential consequences of withdrawal from the agreement*. Ann Arbor: Center for Automotive Research.

EYGM. (2017, February 3). *USA New Government: Implications for the Mexican automotive industry*. EY Report. http://www.ey.com/Publication/vwLUAssets/ey-usa-new-government-implications-for-the-mexican-automotive-industry/$FILE/ey-usa-new-government-implications-for-the-mexican-automotive-industry.pdf Accessed 13 Sept 2017.

Global Business Reports. (2016). *Mexico's regional automotive report 2016*. Singapore: Global Business Reports.

Granados, U. (2016, November–December). Mexico and Japan, coping with the multilateral trade crisis. *Negocios Promexico,* pp. 16–19.

JBIC. (2016). *Survey report on overseas business operations by Japanese manufacturing companies*. Retrieved from http://www.jbic.go.jp/en

JETRO. (2017). *Japan's outward and inward foreign direct investment*. Retrieved from https://www.jetro.go.jp/en/reports/statistics/

Lichtensztejn, S. (2014). La Inversión Extranjera Directa en México (1980-2011) Aspectos Cuantitativos y Cualitativos. In S. Lichtensztejn (coord.). *Inversión Extranjera en Países Emergentes en Transición*. Mexico: Universidad Veracruzana.

Magaña, O. (2016, November–December). Production must go on. *Negocios Promexico,* pp. 28–29.

METI. (2017). *Quarterly survey of overseas subsidiaries*. Retrieved from http://www.meti.go.jp/english/statistics/tyo/genntihou/index.html

OECD. (2017). *OECD.Stat*. Retrieved from http://stats.oecd.org/

Promexico. (2016). *The Mexican automotive industry: Current situation, challenges and opportunities*. Mexico: Proméxico.

Salas, B. (2016, November–December). Japanese companies in Mexico set to top 1,000. *Negocios Promexico,* pp. 10–13.

SE. (2017). *Competitividad y Normatividad/Inversión Extranjera Directa*. Retrieved from http://www.gob.mx/se/

Chapter 2
Japanese Foreign Direct Investment in Mexico's Transport Equipment Sector. The Macro Impact: Regional Networks of Production and Trade

Melba Falck-Reyes

Abstract In the past 15 years, Mexico has been favored by increasing flows of Foreign Direct Investment (FDI), being the Japanese source one of the most important. The chapter analyzes the impact of Japanese FDI in Mexico at the macro-level with emphasis on the impact of Japanese FDI on Mexico's trade flows and on the formation of regional networks in the Transport Equipment sector (TE), especially within the North American Region. This study is carried out under the Fragmentation of Production Theory approach, which emphasizes the role of Multinational firms (MN) in international trade based on the new organization of production among plants in different countries. The analysis is based on database that classifies trade flows by main stages of production that allow assessing trade in intermediate goods and also on information on local and regional content of Japanese automotive brands assembled in Mexico. The results indicate that Japanese FDI in Mexico has contributed notably to the formation on production networks in North America in the TE sector.

Keywords Japan · Mexico · North America · Foreign direct investment · Networks of production · Intermediate goods trade · Transport equipment sector

2.1 Introduction

In the past 15 years, Mexico has been favored by increasing flows of FDI, being the Japanese source one of the most important. The spur of Japanese investment has more than doubled between the years 2011 and 2016, increasing the number of Japanese companies in the country to more than one thousand. Moreover, of the total investment announced by Japanese companies in the past 12 years, about two thirds were concentrated on automobile and auto-parts sectors.

M. Falck-Reyes (✉)
Pacific Studies Department, University of Guadalajara, Zapopan, Mexico
e-mail: mefalck@gmail.com

M. Falck-Reyes, L. Guzman-Anaya (eds.), *Japanese Direct Investment in Mexico's Transport Equipment Sector*, New Frontiers in Regional Science: Asian Perspectives 22,
https://doi.org/10.1007/978-981-10-7718-0_2

Several factors have contributed to this inflow of Japanese investment: the network of Free Trade Agreements (FTA) signed by Mexico (12 with 46 countries), including the Japan-Mexico Economic Partnership Agreement (JMEPA); potential growth of domestic and neighboring foreign markets (North America and Latin American countries); the network of suppliers already established in Mexico and the supply of skilled labor force, among others.[1]

The Japanese flows of investment through the networks of production have had an important impact at the macro level by affecting the flows of intra-regional and inter-regional trade of Mexico. At the same time they have had important effects on the gradual development of networks of local suppliers and on the demand and training of human resources at the local level. Local governments, especially in the central region of Mexico (the Mexican Bajío), where flows of investment had been intense, had responded with public policies to promote the investment flow.[2] Cooperation among the Federal Government, local governments, Japanese companies, the Japan International Cooperation Agency (JICA) and the Japan External Trade Organization (JETRO) had been key parts to facilitate these flows of investment.[3]

Considering that Mexico has become the 4th main exporter of automobiles and the 7th major producer in the world, Japanese investment in the TE has become a key factor contributing to those outcomes. The results presented in this chapter analyze the impact of Japanese FDI in Mexico at the macro-level with emphasis on the impact of Japanese FDI on the formation of regional networks in the TE sector, especially within the North American Region, and their impact on México's trade. Other chapters of the book analyze the local responses to the FDI of Japan.

This chapter is organized in the following sections. The first one is an overview of the Fragmentation of Production Theory. The next ones analyze the boom of Japanese investment in Mexico and the way Japanese affiliates are operating in networks of production in the TE sector. The next section constitutes de core of the chapter as it focus on empirical evidence on how Japanese FDI has influenced the patterns of current Mexico's trade flows and how it has contributed to the formation of the network of production in the TE sector in North America. The next section is devoted to the challenges that Mexico faces under this new scheme of production. Conclusions close the chapter.

---

[1] Look at the Chap. 3 by Leo Guzman-Anaya for a more detailed account of Localization factors of Japanese investment in Mexico.

[2] See Chap. 5 by Maria Guadalupe Lugo-Sanchez to have a deeper look at the public policies carried out by the local governments of the Bajío region to foster investment.

[3] See Chap. 6 by Leo Guzman-Anaya for the role of Training Programs (TPs) carried out by JICA as mechanisms for technological and knowledge transfer to local firms and the productivity gains from these programs.

2.2 Fragmentation of Production Theory

This study is carried out under the Fragmentation of Production Theory approach, which emphasizes the role of MNs in international trade based on the new organization of production among plants in different countries as a result of improvements in transportation and new developments in Information, Communications and Technology (ICT) (Baldwin et al. 2013:1–15; Yamashita 2010:5–28). Under this framework, Global chains of production have important impacts in the nature of trade. Nowadays trade in intermediate goods has intensified as firms choose to procure their inputs in local and international markets and this behavior in turn has important effects on the recipient country of foreign investment. Moreover, sales strategies of final goods by global value chains also have an impact in the direction of trade of the recipient country. In this manner, foreign investment and trade are closely interwoven.

Supported on empirical evidence from Asian networks of production, Kimura and Ando (2006) developed a conceptual framework, based on firm-level decisions, to understand firm's choices regarding location of process of production in different places. According to their study, distance and controllability are the main variables that determine costs of firms fragmenting their production. A well-established hub of parts and components suppliers, lower wages and appropriate infrastructure in the recipient countries can compensate costs related to displacement of production. These ideas had been further developed by Head and Mayer (2016), who identify another important aspect to be taking into consideration by firms when deciding fragmenting their production, namely the separation from brand's headquarters. These authors base their analysis at the level of brands and models to understand firm's decisions regarding in which markets offer a determined brand and from which countries source specific inputs to each brand.

As these tendencies have intensified, the response of recipient countries to maximize their welfare from the incoming investment has to do with how to design industrial policies to accommodate and take advantage of these new ways of international production. How local Small and Medium Enterprises (SME), engage in global chains of production becomes a very important aspect for the recipient country to share the benefits of increasing trade propelled by inward investment. As has been pointed by Baldwin and Okubo (2012) in their networked model of investment, the challenge for countries to attain a higher level of development is not to develop a whole sector of the economy, but to take advantage of the existing network of production promoted by MNs in the recipient country and to incorporate national suppliers to the chain of production.

This chapter aims to study the complex network of relations, both intraregional in the North American region and interregional with Asian countries that the Japanese FDI in Mexico has encouraged. It will look closer to the relationship between FDI and trade flows fostered by the new fragmentation of production being carried out by Japanese Multinationals. The TE sector is used as a case of study because of importance in Mexican exports and in the Mexican economy. It comprises both the automotive components and the Automotive Original Equipment Manufacturing (OEM) sub-sectors. The data utilized to assess the impact of Japanese investment on Mexico's international trade is based on the data-base (RIETI-TID) published by the Research Institute of Economy Trade and Industry (RIETI) of Japan that classifies trade flows into three main stages of production: primary goods, intermediate goods and final goods. Intermediate goods in turn are divided in two sub-categories of processed goods and parts and components while the final goods category includes capital and consumption goods. Unfortunately RIETI ended publishing a database that presented information at firm level on Japanese affiliates business activities regarding sales and procurement. The last one available is the 2010 that covered until 2006. As a closer substitute, though not as comprehensive as RIETI's, I am using information regarding local and regional procurement of Japanese brands of cars assembled in Mexico and in the United States (US). These data is being published by the Department of Transportation of the US.

2.3 Trade Balance and Investment: Two Sides of the Same Coin

During the eighties, given the high value of the Yen and also the high-cost structure in the domestic economy, Japanese companies lost competitiveness in the international markets and they reacted investing heavily abroad making Japan one of the major investors in the world. Japanese companies were looking for efficiency costs in Asia and to overcome trade barriers in the US. By the end of the decade, Japan became the engine of the networked production in Asia (Lakhera 2008:28–31; Falck-Reyes 2015:57–68). During the nineties, Mexico became an attractive place to invest since the Free Trade Agreement with North America (NAFTA) signed in 1994, made the country an attractive platform to export to the US market.

Ten years after NAFTA, Mexico and Japan signed their EPA. Both countries were seeking to improve their competitiveness at the international markets where the incorporation of China to the World Trade Organization (WTO) posed a new challenge.[4] Since NAFTA, Mexico had signed several Free Trade Agreements, including one with the European Union, but none with a country in Asia. Hence, Japan became the first country in Asia with which Mexico had an EPA and still is. For Japan, the Mexican EPA was the second agreement signed, being the first one with Singapore. Since then, flows of trade and investment grew steadily between the two countries. Exports have more than doubled while imports have increased by 64%. Currently (2015) total trade between the two countries amounts 22 billion dollars showing a deficit of about 12 billion dollars for Mexico (Fig. 2.1).

[4] See Ministry of Foreign Affairs of Japan (2002), I participated in this Group as part of the Mexican Academic Group.

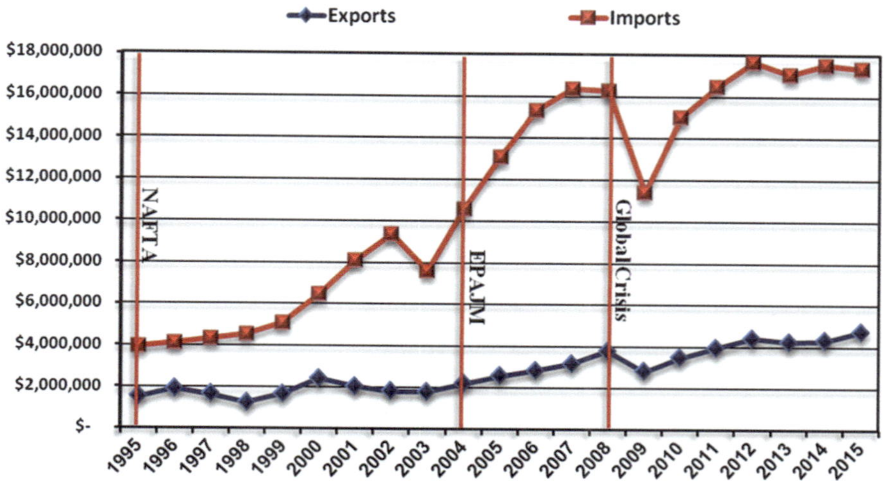

Fig. 2.1 Mexico and Japan: evolution of exports and imports. 1995–2015
Thousands of US dollars
Source: Own elaboration with information of Mexico's Ministry of Economy for data related to imports and JETRO-Mexico with information from the Ministry of Finance of Japan, for data related to exports to Japan
http://www.economia-snci.gob.mx/
https://www.jetro.go.jp/mexico/

However, the above figure doesn't give the whole picture of the economic relationship between Mexico and Japan. These trade flows are closely related to the direct investment carried out by Japanese MNs in Mexico. Moreover, Japanese FDI is not only affecting the bilateral economic relationship, but also Mexican trade flows with other regions, namely, North America and Asia.

In fact, if we look at Fig. 2.2, it shows a growing surplus of Mexico with NAFTA countries of about 100 billion dollars mirrored by a growing deficit with East Asia (Japan, China and South Korea) and a steady and smaller one with the Europe. And here is where Japanese investment enters the picture. On the one hand, Japanese MNs established in Mexico participated in an important way to exports from Mexico to the NAFTA countries, especially to the US, contributing notably to the Mexican surplus balance of trade with that region. Japanese MNs established in Mexico make one of every three automobiles exported to the US (Secretaría de Economía and ProMéxico 2015). On the other hand, Japanese MNs operating in Mexico had spurred imports of intermediate goods not only from Japan, but also from other countries in Asia, contributing in that way to the deficit that Mexico has with that region. Let's look more closely to the recent flows of investment from Japan into Mexico.

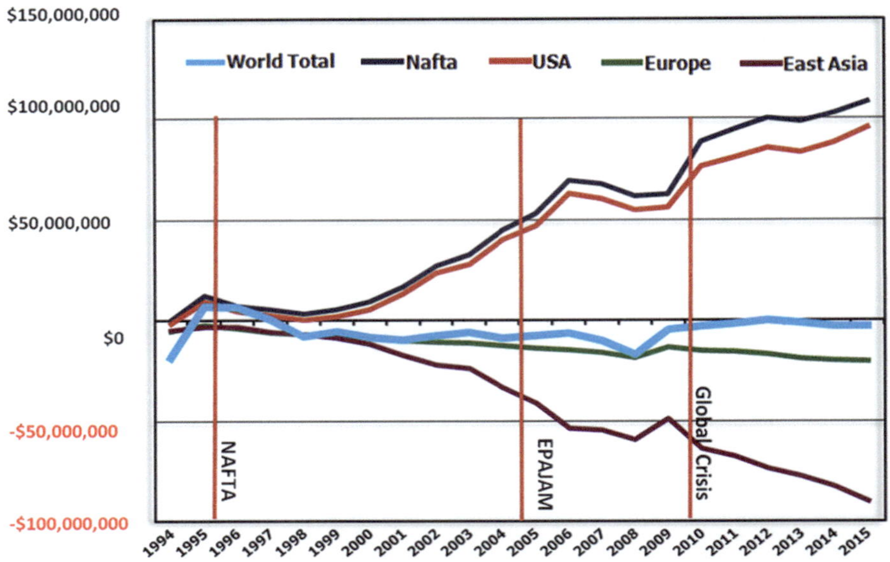

Fig. 2.2 Mexico: evolution of trade balance by main regions. 1995–2015
Thousands of US dollars
Source: Own elaboration with information from RIETI-TID 2015 and Mexico's Ministry of Economy
http://www.rieti-tid.com/trade.php
http://www.gob.mx/se/

2.4 The Boom of Japanese Investment in Mexico

Japanese investment has had presence in Mexico since the sixties, when the Maquiladora Program established by the Mexican government to promote exports to the US attracted some Japanese companies. Nissan was the first one to arrive in 1959 as distributor and by 1966 started its production. It was the first plant to establish operations outside Japan.[5] At that time, Border States with the US received the major flows of investment (Secretaría de Economía and ProMéxico 2015:52–55). The eighties witnessed a spur of Japanese outflows of investment to the world but not to Latin American countries. At the time this region was under a severe economic crisis and Mexico was not the exception (Kuwayama 2015:19–23). However during this decade, Japanese companies started investing in the US in order to overcome the restrictions that the US government was placing on Japanese exports of cars to that market. In the nineties, with NAFTA, Japanese companies started to look back at Mexico as a platform to export to the US and increased their investment in this country (Interamerican Development Bank 2013:3–35). But it was only after Mexico and Japan signed the EPA in 2004, when Japanese investment started to explode.

[5] Look at Chap. 4 by Emma Mendoza that focuses on the demonstration effect from Japanese firms located within the State of Aguascalientes and the role of Nissan.

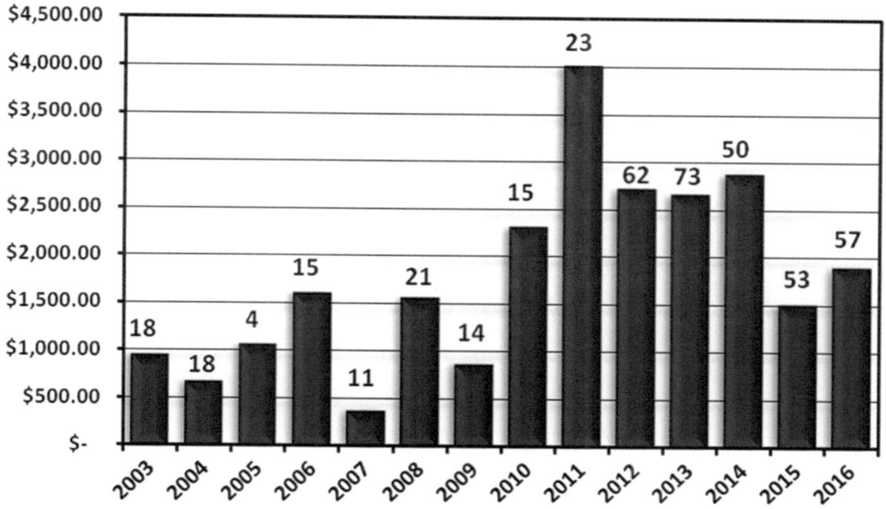

Fig. 2.3 Mexico: flows of FDI and projects announced by Japanese companies. 2003–2016
Flows of investment in Millions of US dollars
Number of projects on top of each column
Source: Own elaboration with information from The Financial Times (2017) fDiMarkets.com Trends Report: FDI from Japan to Mexico. January 2003 to June 2017

In fact, between the years 2003 and 2016 Japanese companies have announced more than 400 investment projects in Mexico, 68% of which were announced in the past 5 years (Fig. 2.3). The total amount involved is 26 billion dollars of which about half has already been invested. Moreover, it is the Transport Equipment sector the one that has been favored by the greatest number of projects (44%) and the amount of investment announced (62%).

The central region of El Bajío in Mexico has been the major destination for Japanese companies. The states of Guanajuato, Aguascalientes, Querétaro, San Luis Potosi and Jalisco have attracted about 60% of the investing companies. Hence this region is becoming a major cluster for the Transport Equipment sector in Mexico (See Map 2.1). In the North, the States of Nuevo León and Baja California had been also major beneficiaries of Japanese investment during this boom.

The main global Japan's OEMs have presence in Mexico: Nissan, Honda, Mazda and Toyota and they have been followed by a plethora of parts and components manufacturers. The number of the Japanese companies in the country has more than doubled in the past 5 years. By the end of 2016, there were more than one thousand Japanese affiliates operating in Mexico, as reported by the director of Jetro-Mexico, Tadashi Mineura (Juárez 2017).

Besides the impact of the amounts invested (about 70% are new investments), Japanese investment in Mexico is having important effects on employment. In general, the level of employment in the TE sector in Mexico has increased notably in the past 10 years from 500 thousand employed persons in 2007 to 800 thousand in

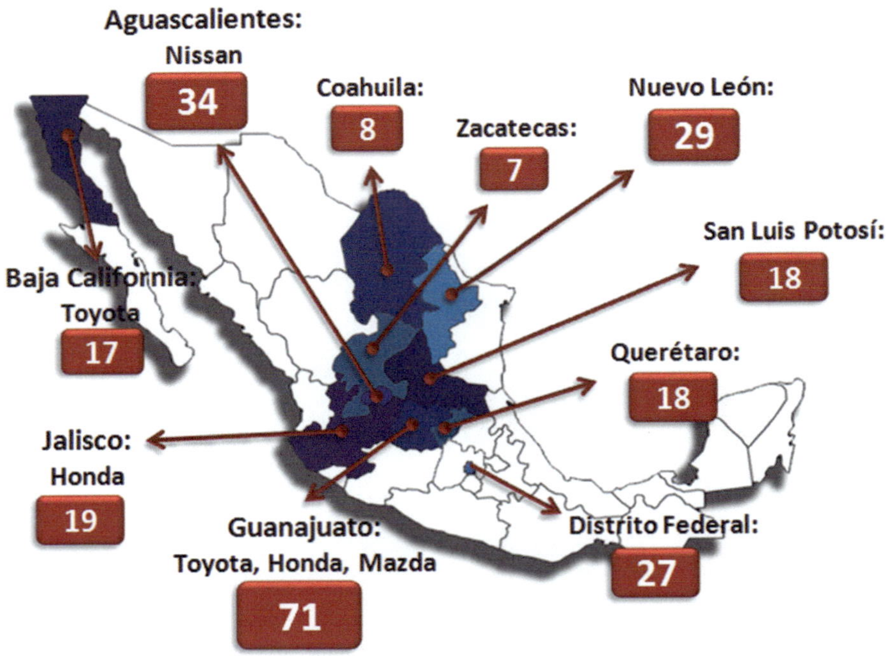

Map 2.1 Location of Japanese affiliates in Mexico. 2015
Numbers represent the Japanese affiliates operating in the selected states
Source: Own elaboration with information of the Secretariat of Economy Mexico and JETRO-Mexico. http://www.gob.mx/se/
https://www.jetro.go.jp/mexico/

2016 (Fig. 2.4). Most of this jobs are direct employment and are originated in the Auto Parts industry (90%) (Negocios ProMéxico 2015:20). Moreover, in the Commerce and Services sub-sector, where there are 1972 automotive distribution agencies, 490, thousand jobs are created (AMIA et al. 2016). Regarding the role of Japanese investment announced on employment, it is projected that it will create more than 127 thousand jobs and that the Transport Equipment Sector will generate about 65% of those (fDiMarkets.com 2017). This figure represents 16% of the current total employment of the Transport Equipment Sector in Mexico. Let's turn now to the impact of Japanese investment on the trade sector of Mexico.

According to the International Organization of Motor Vehicles Manufacturers (OICA) (2015), currently Mexico produces 3.5 million motor vehicles, which represent 20% of the production of the NAFTA countries (US 67.5% and Canada 12.5%). Thus, Mexico has become the 7th largest producer of automobiles in the world and the fourth major exporter. Accompanying this trend, the auto parts sector has increased considerable. For the economy, the TE sector represents 17% of the Manufacturing Gross Domestic Product (GDP), 20% of FDI and one third of total exports. Mexico is also the leading supplier of Auto Parts to the US (Negocios ProMéxico 2015:18–21). According to INEGIs' database on the Profile of

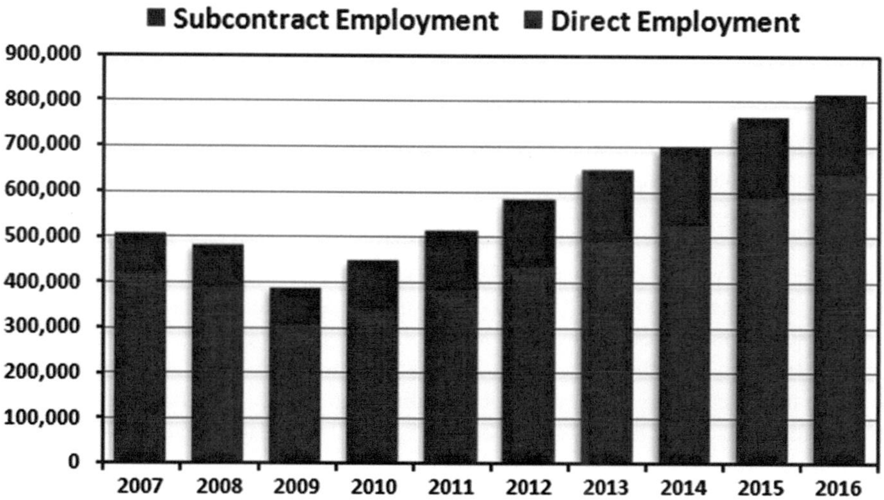

Fig. 2.4 Mexico: evolution of employment in the transport equipment sector. 2007–2016 Number of jobs by main category
Source: Own elaboration with information of INEGI Mexico www.inegi.org.mx

Manufacturing Exporting Companies (2015) there are in the TE sector 730 exporters that represent 12% of the total for the country. The biggest companies, those with more than 250 employees, concentrate TE exports. This group, comprised of 444 enterprises contributes with 98% of the exports of automotive and auto parts goods. Given the economies of scale requirements for international trade, SMEs play a minor role as exporters. That is why, it is important for the host country of investment flows to develop a strategy to incorporate SMEs as suppliers of global value chains.

2.5 How Japanese Affiliates Are Operating in Mexico?

Now, in order to assess the impact of Japanese affiliates operating in Mexico it is important to take into consideration the way MNs organize their production nowadays. Both, the development of information technology and of the communications systems as already mentioned, has enabled the manufacturers to organize their production in such a way that the inputs required for the final product can be obtained from different locations in the world. So, the firm has a different set of input sources: domestic or foreign procurement. Furthermore, in the domestic market a firm can source its inputs from local suppliers or from foreign suppliers established in the domestic market. Whereas supply in foreign markets, can be located in the same region where the host country is located or in different regions. The transactions carried out by firms sourcing inputs can be intra-firm, inter-firm or in the market at large. Regarding sales, the firm target markets can be the domestic market of the host country or foreign markets situated in the same region of the host-country or in a different region.

When foreign firms operate in this manner they develop a "networked investment", as Baldwin and Okubo (2012) have coined the term. And this networked investment has important impacts on flows of trade of the host country. If the main source of inputs is foreign, imports of intermediate goods (parts and components) will tend to increase. If the domestic market is the main supplier, imports of intermediate goods will tend to decrease. For sales, if foreign markets are the main target of the MNs, then exports of final goods will tend to increase. And if a cluster of inputs suppliers is well established in the host country, exports of intermediate goods will also tend to increase. Under this framework of production, companies have to take a complex set of choices regarding trade costs, coordination costs and marketing costs, what Head and Mayer (2015) have labeled the Triangle of Frictions in firm's production and selling decisions.

According to the last Basic Survey of Japanese Affiliates Business Activities carried out by the Ministry of Economy and Trade of Japan, in 2015 there were 25,233 Japanese affiliates operating abroad, 66% of them located in Asia and a third of those in China. In North America (US and Canada) there were 3268 Japanese affiliates and 1111 in Mexico (Juárez 2017). According to the same survey of Japanese affiliates, almost half of them are located in manufacturing industries of which TE sector is the most important with 21% of affiliates located on it; this is followed by information and communication and electronics equipment and chemicals sectors. Of the 5.6 million people employed by Japanese overseas affiliates, 80% of them are located in the manufacturing sector and of those, 37% are localized in the TE sector. As mentioned above, since the eighties the revaluation of the Yen and the high domestic cost structure in Japan plus the stagnation of the economy in the last two decades had prompted Japanese companies to relocate their production abroad. The result is that 38.9% of the total production of Japanese companies with affiliates is being carried out overseas, whereas back in 2004 the same production ratio was 29.9%. This tendency is more acute in the TE sector where the overseas production ratio is 48.8% up from 36% a decade ago.

Considering the web of Japanese affiliates operating in North America and Mexico (4379) and being Japan the major investor from Asia in manufacturing industries in Mexico and the second major investor in the TE sector in the country, the flows of intermediate goods between Mexico, Japan and Rest of Asia and North America are closely linked to this networked investment. The dotted lines in Diagram 2.1 indicate the number of Japanese affiliates operating in Asia, Mexico and North America in 2015. The solid arrows represent Mexico's relations with those regions/countries in intermediate goods. In that year, imports of intermediate goods from Japan into Mexico were almost 10 billion dollars, 19% of which corresponded to the TE sector. While exports of the same types of goods from Mexico to Japan were more than one billion dollars, of which 12% are part of the TE sector. Moreover, Mexico imported from Asia without Japan, 54 billion dollars of intermediate goods, mainly from China and South Korea (81%) and 9% corresponded to the

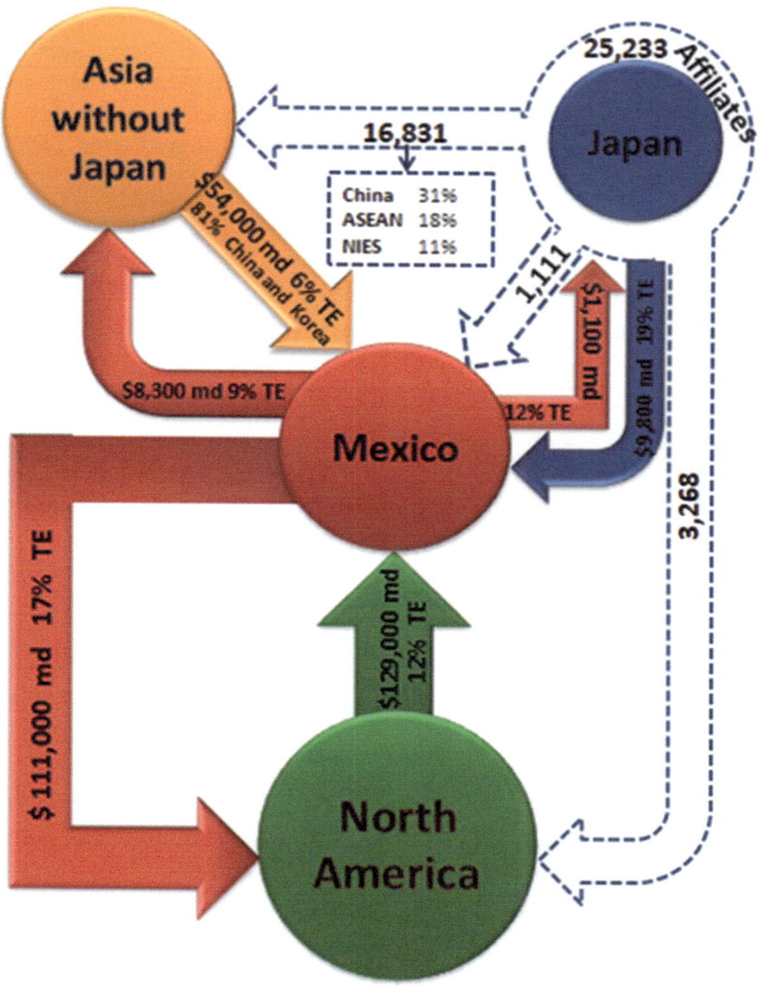

Diagram 2.1 Japanese affiliates operating in Asia and North America and flows of intermediate goods 2015
Source: Own elaboration with information from RIETI-TID 2015 and the Summary of the 46th Survey on Overseas Business Activities, 2016
http://www.rieti-tid.com/trade.php
http://www.meti.go.jp/english/statistics/tyo/kaigaizi/index.html
Note: *ASEAN* Association of South East Asian Nations, *NIES* New Industrialized Countries

TE sector. Whereas Mexico exports of intermediate goods to this region were 8.3 billion dollars and 9% of those corresponded to the TE sector.

With North America, Mexico's trade on intermediate goods is stronger. Mexico's imports from this region amounted to more than 129 billion dollars in 2015 with the TE sector representing 12%. Mexico's exports of the same type of goods were 111 billion dollars with the TE sector representing 17%. These figures are an example of the new tendencies that characterize trade in the twenty-first century: greater intensity of intra-industry trade in intermediate goods between developed and developing countries (Baldwin 2016). And in the case of Mexico is being fostered, in part, by the presence of Japanese MNs in the country and their respective hubs of production, both in Asia and North America.

2.6 Empirical Evidence: Influence of Japanese FDI in Mexico's Flows of Trade and Regional Networks of Production

But Diagram 2.1 gives us a picture of just one year. Let's look more closely to the tendency of the Mexican flows of imports of intermediate goods by regions since the signing of NAFTA, and a clearer picture emerges of the above-mentioned influence of Japanese FDI. Using data prepared by RIETI, that as already noted classifies flows of trade based on the stages of production, Figure 2.5 shows that from year 1995 up to 2000, NAFTA countries, and mainly the US supplied almost 80% of Mexico's intermediate goods imports. However, since the beginning of this century, NAFTA had been losing relative importance as a supplier of intermediate goods (54%). Europe has maintained a stable share as supplier of intermediate goods with

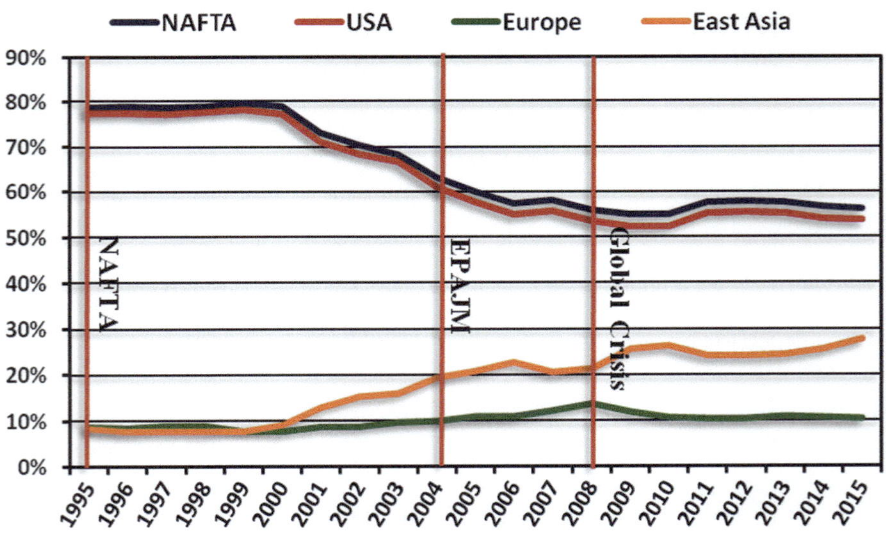

Fig. 2.5 Mexico: evolution of imports of intermediate goods. Share by main regions. 1995–2015 Percentages (%)
Source: Own elaboration with information from RIETI-TID 2015. http://www.rieti-tid.com/trade.php

10% participation. Instead, East Asia (Japan, South Korea and China) had gained importance increasing their relative share from 8% in 1995 to 28% in 2015, supplying now 64 billion in those types of goods to Mexico.

Turning to the TE sector, the evolution of imports of intermediate goods by regions shows that the relative importance of NAFTA as a supplier has also decreased from 81% in 1995 to 67% in 2015, whereas East Asia has increased its participation as a supplier of intermediate goods to the TE sector from 6% in 1995 to 21% in 2015 (Fig. 2.6). It must be noted though that in this particular sector, NAFTA's relative share is greater than that on the intermediate goods in general. Behind this result is, most probably, the fact that there are 3268 Japanese affiliates operating in the US and Canada (Diagram 2.1) that are also suppliers of intermediate goods to the Mexican market. According to the report "FDI from the US to Mexico", from fDi markets (2017), during the period between years 2013 to 2017, 559 projects were announced by Japanese companies related to the Automotive Components sector and the Automotive OEMs sector. The total amount announced to be invested was 30 billion dollars, one third of total inward investment from Japan to the US. Job creation was estimated in 91 thousand. Hence, estimated capital investment per job in the US was 329 thousand dollars compared to 192 thousand dollars in Mexico, where investment is more intensive in labor. Toyota, Honda, Nissan, Toyota Motor, Subaru America and Bridgestone Americas Tire Operations, were among the top ten companies investing in the US in this period. From this information, it can be inferred that the Japanese affiliates operating in the US and Mexico have contributed to the spur of the intermediate goods in trade in general and in the TE sector trough inter-firm, intra-firm and trade at length.

However, to have a more accurate picture of the network of transactions in the intermediate goods for the TE sector, it is necessary to have a firm-level analysis of Japanese affiliates operating in Japan and North America. Unfortunately, RIETI ceased to produce such data- base, as mentioned above. Therefore, as a second best choice, I use data from the US Department of Transportation related to different brands of automobiles being sold in the US market that contains information of final assembly country and local and foreign content of parts and components.

According to this source both, Mexico and Japan are important suppliers of different brands of motor vehicles being sold in the US, ranking third and fourth by the number of brands sold, after Germany and the US (NHTS). Panel A of Fig. 2.7, shows local (left panel), regional (right panel) and foreign procurement ratios for 14 Japanese brands of motor vehicles sold in the US market and having Mexico as the final Assembly country. Panel B shows the same information for 36 Japanese brands that have the US as a final Assembly country. In the case of Mexico, in eight of the fourteen models, local procurement ratio is 60% and mainly foreign countries supply the rest. But if we look at right Panel A, regional procurement increases between 5% and 25%, placing regional content average at 66% compared to 52% average local content. Procurement coming outside the region is mainly from Japan and other Asian countries. Thus, of the 14 Japanese brands, the engine is supplied evenly between Mexico and Japan, whereas the transmission sources are Mexico (5), Japan (6), Philippines (2) and China (1).

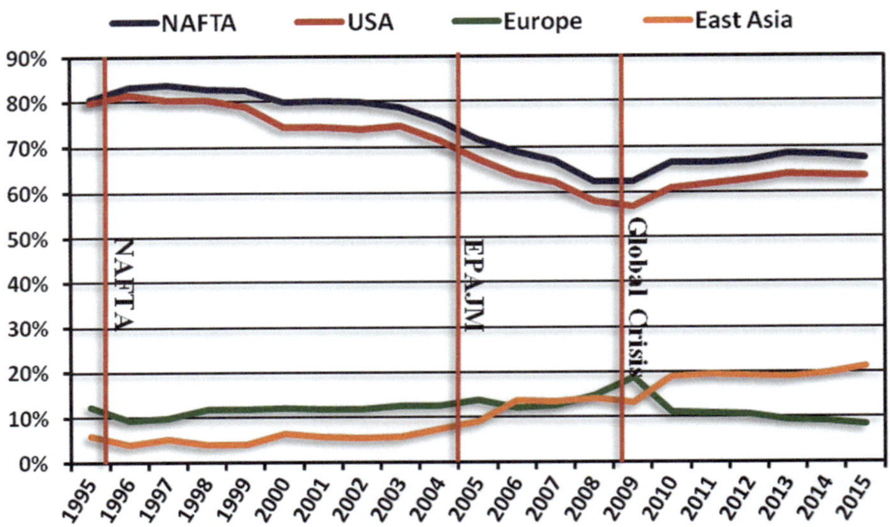

Fig. 2.6 Mexico: evolution of imports of intermediate goods in the transport equipment sector. Share by main regions. 1995–2015
Percentages (%)
Source: Own elaboration with information from RIETI-TID 2015.
http://www.rieti-tid.com/trade.php

In the case of Japanese brands that have as a final Assembly country the US (Panel B), 21 of the 36 brands have a local procurement ratio between 60% and 80%, and 9 more brands have a local procurement ratio between 50% and 55%. Therefore Japanese brands being assembled in the US use a greater percentage of local content than the ones being assembled in Mexico. Hence local and regional content almost coincide. In 6 brands Mexico supplies the transmission. Foreign procurement is coming from Japan and South Korea mainly. Of the 36 brands, in five cases the engine is supplied by Japan and in 14 cases the transmission is supplied by that country.

In sum, Japanese affiliates operating in Mexico according to their sources of procurement, are having an important impact on Mexican imports of intermediate goods in the TE sector: relative share of East Asian countries has increased to 21% mainly from China, Japan and South Korea, countries in which there are Japanese affiliates operating; NAFTA countries, in particular the US, continue to be major suppliers of auto parts though their share has diminished to 67% from 80% in the nineties. Taking into consideration that there are more than 3000 Japanese affiliates operating in US and Canada, it is safe to assume that they also have an important share on this trade. These results are consistent with the ratios of local and foreign procurement of Japanese vehicles brands sold in the US market with Mexico and US as final assembly countries.

To complete the above analysis, let's look at the Mexico's flow of exports in the TE sector by main regions of destination. As can be seen in Fig. 2.8, NAFTA countries are the main destination for final goods in the TE equipment sector. The value

Panel A: Mexico Final Assembly country

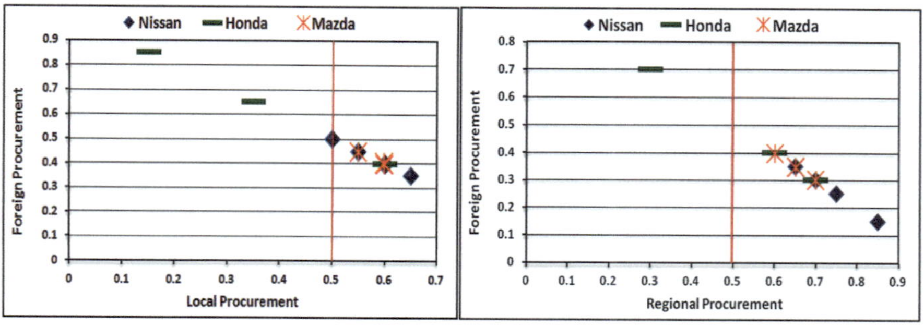

Panel B: US Final Assembly country

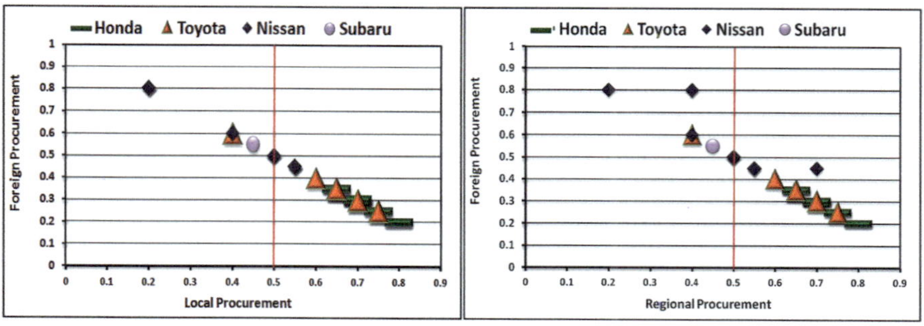

Fig. 2.7 Japanese brands of motor vehicles sold in the US market by final assembly country. Local, regional and foreign procurement ratios. 2016
Percentages (%)
Source: Own elaboration with data from NHTSA, U.S. Department of Transportation, National Highway Traffic Safety Administration. http://www.nhtsa.gov/

of this category of exports, since the signature of NAFTA agreement, has increased by six times, reaching a level of almost 60 billion dollars in 2015. It must be noted the acceleration of the growth rate of this category of exports since the financial crisis of 2008. Thus, more than 80% of final goods of the TE sector are exported by Mexico to NAFTA countries and one third of the automobiles exported by Mexico are manufactured by Japanese OEMs operating in Mexico. The remainder is exported, by order of importance, to Europe, Mercosur and East Asia.

Regarding exports of intermediate goods (auto parts and components), they represent now 30% of the total exports of TE sector. The value of this type of exports has increased steadily since NAFTA from 2.8 billion in 1995 to 25 billion dollars in 2015 (Fig. 2.9). They also have showed the same tendency as final goods growing at an accelerated rate after the financial crisis. By regions, 90% of these exports have NAFTA countries as destination (US 82%); the remainder 10% is going to East Asia (4%), Europe (3%) and Mercosur (2%). These trade patterns of exports and imports of intermediate goods in the TE sector concentrated mainly in the NAFTA

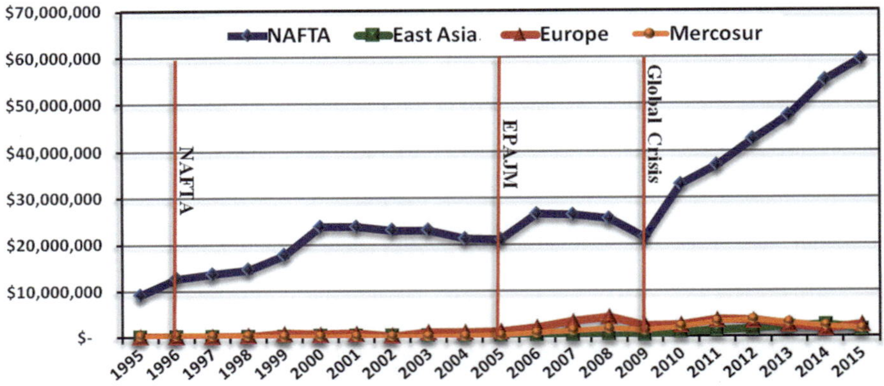

Fig. 2.8 Mexico: evolution of exports of final goods in transport equipment sector by main regions. 1995–2015
Thousands of US dollars
Source: Own elaboration with information from RIETI-TID 2015
http://www.rieti-tid.com/trade.php

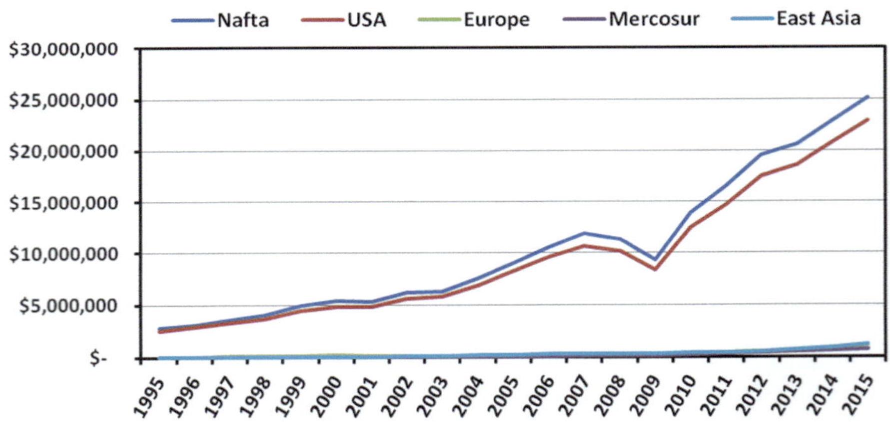

Fig. 2.9 Mexico: evolution of exports of intermediate goods in transport equipment sector by main regions. 1995–2015
Thousands of US dollars
Source: Own elaboration with information from RIETI-TID 2015.
http://www.rieti-tid.com/trade.php

region, are indicative of the network of production that has been established and that more than 4000 thousand Japanese affiliates operating in the same region are contributing to such integration of production. These results have been facilitated by the signature of trade agreements among NAFTA countries and between Japan and Mexico which had given preferential treatment to flows of trade and investment.

As a result of these tendencies, the trade surplus in the TE sector of Mexico with NAFTA countries has multiplied by five times since the signature of NAFTA, reach-

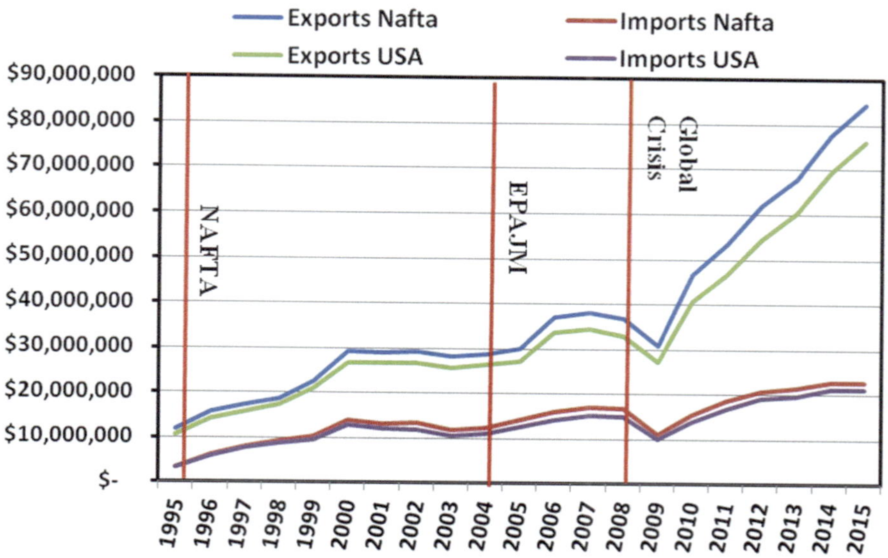

Fig. 2.10 Mexico: evolution of trade balance in the transportation equipment sector. 1995–2015 Thousands of US dollars
Source: Own elaboration with information from RIETI-TID 2015. http://www.rieti-tid.com/trade.php

ing currently a level of 61.7 billion and of those 55 billion are a surplus with the US (Fig. 2.10). Therefore, the TE sector has had a very important role in the total surplus of Mexico with the US, as it represents 57% of the total surplus with that country and Japanese affiliates are playing an important role on generating it.

2.7 Major Challenges for Mexico Under the New Scheme of Production Networks

What the preceding analysis shows is that the patterns of exports and imports in the TE sector of Mexico are indicative of the regional network of production established in NAFTA where 4000 Japanese affiliates operating in the region are contributing to such integration of production.

One of the main challenges for Mexico, as a recipient country of these flows of investment, is how to incorporate local SMEs into the regional chains of production. According to the Asia-Pacific Economic Cooperation (APEC) Supporting Industry Report on Mexico in the automotive industry of the country there are 20 foreign OEMs at the top of the production pyramid which are served by 350 Tier 1 auto parts suppliers that operate 600 plants, most of them being foreign companies. At the base of the pyramid are 400 Tier 2 companies, 30% of them Mexican and 2,290 companies forming the Tier 3 auto parts suppliers, mainly by medium size Mexican companies. These companies are involved in machining, assembly, stamping, welding, plastic injection and smelting, among other activities (APEC 2017:20). However, as is pointed out by the President of the National Autoparts Industry (INA), "SMEs suppliers are short term oriented and lack competitiveness" (Negocios ProMéxico 2015:46–47).

Moreover, it is recognized by the most representatives' organizations of TE sector that among the main challenges for the Mexican Automotive sector are the need to strength local support industries and linked to that, to strength the educative system in order to increase the labor force capabilities (AMIA et al. 2016). In this regard, JICA and JETRO in Mexico had been working for several years now to develop local domestic suppliers with the Ministry of Economy and the local and state governments of the recipient localities of Japanese FDI[6] (Secretaría de Economía and ProMéxico 2015:44–49), but the progress had been slow. Another aspect that had been mentioned by the Japanese affiliates operating in Mexico is the need for training of human capital. Universities and Technical Institutes had also been working with recipient localities,[7] but given the increasing demand of specialized human resources, companies are experiencing shortage of those resources.

Currently the main challenge for the network of firms operating in the TE sector in the North American region is the new wave of protectionism in the United States. Uncertainty is the main feature at this conjecture. Nowadays, the three countries that integrate the NAFTA are in their second round of negotiations. The salient feature regarding the TE sector, and where President Trump has concentrated its pressure, is related to the Rules of Origin. Under the present scheme, the TE sector has to fulfill 62.5% of regional content for goods exported/imported to receive preferential treatment (Villarreal and Fergusson 2017). The US is proposing to increase the regional content. In that case intermediate inputs imported from other countries, mainly from Asia, will decrease. This will tend to increase costs and make the industry in general, less competitive. The other way out is to attract more auto-parts suppliers from abroad to be established in Mexico and/or develop more local national suppliers, but that will take time.

The other possible scenario under the current level of affairs is that NAFTA cease to operate. In that case, the three countries must abide by the WTO rules. And under this organization's rules, as asymmetry is recognized, the US will confront higher tariffs than Mexico. A third possibility that has been considered by President Trump is to set 35% tariffs on Mexican imports.[8] Head and Mayer (2016) had made estimations of the negative impact of this measure, assuming that Mexico will retaliate with the same level of tariffs. They estimate a drop in production by 40% in Mexico, being this the worst scenario.

In the end, given the full integration of value chains under NAFTA, and especially in the TE sector, this "reverse integration" a term coined by Head and Mayer

---

[6] See Chap. 6 by Leo Guzman-Anaya on the role that JICA is playing to train local suppliers.

[7] See Chap. 4 on Spillovers of Japanese Automotive Companies' Activities in the State of Aguascalientes by Emma Mendoza in this book.

[8] Though lately it has not been mentioned by the US negotiators of NAFTA.

(2016), will increase US intermediate good's prices and will affect negatively competitiveness of US final goods in international markets. Moreover, domestic prices will also rise. In the end, producers of parts and components in the US will be negatively affected and with the loss of market, employment will suffer. Therefore, it will not be an easy task to dismantle such a network of regional production and the consequences would be negative to all participants.

2.8 Conclusions

As has been discussed along the chapter, the patterns of exports and imports in the TE sector, both in final and intermediate goods, are indicative of the regional network of production in NAFTA. As more than 4000 thousand Japanese affiliates operate in the region, they have contributed notably to the integration of production. Japanese affiliates have had an important contribution to Mexico's exports of final and intermediate goods to NAFTA countries, especially to the US. At the same time, under the current fragmentation of production, they have contributed to increase imports of intermediate inputs from Asia and North America. In short, Japanese FDI in the TE sector of Mexico is having important impacts on Mexico's trade flows and on the increasing level of employment in the industry.

Moreover, the analysis based on the Japanese brands assembled in Mexico and sold in the US market, show that local procurement supplied either by national companies or by Japanese foreign affiliates (or from other countries) operating in Mexico is more than half of total procurement; if procurement from US and Canada is added, regional content amounts to 66%. Companies established mainly in Asia supply the rest, 34%. Therefore, Japanese affiliates established in Mexico base their procurement decisions on a networked investment pattern, similar to the one described by Baldwin and Okubo, using local, regional and foreign sources of supply of parts and components that form part of the TE sector final goods being exported mainly to regional markets, namely, the US.

For Mexico, one of the main challenges is to incorporate local SMEs into the regional chains of production, in order to share the benefits from Mexico's external sector growth in the past 25 years, now concentrated in few large enterprises. Under the JMEPA, both countries had been cooperating in order to develop local suppliers and that had been another contribution of Japanese FDI in Mexico. But the progress had been slow. Better-coordinated policies are required from part of the Mexican government at Federal and State Level.

Finally, the current state of affairs with the new protectionism from the US, has introduced uncertainty to an otherwise well-functioning network of production in the TE sector in North America to which Japan has contributed considerable.

References

AMIA, AMDA, ANPACT, & INA. (2016). *Diálogo con la industria automotriz 2012–2018*. México: AMIA, Asociación Mexicana de la Industria automotriz; AMDA, Asociación Mexicana de Distribuidores de Automotores; ANPACT, Asociación Nacional de Producción de Autopartes, Camiones y Tractocamiones; INA, Industria Nacional de Autopartes, A.C.

APEC Policy Support Unit. (2017, May). *Supporting industry promotion policies in APEC- Case study on Mexico*. APEC Policy Support Unit. APEC Publications. http://publications.apec.org/file-download.php?filename=217_PSU_Final%20Report_Case%20Study%20on%20Supporting%20Industry_Mexico.pdf&id=1863. Accessed 30 June 2017.

Baldwin, R. (2016). *The great convergence. Information technology and the new globalization*. Cambridge, MA: Harvard University Press.

Baldwin, R., & Okubo, T. (2012). *Networked FDI: Sales and sourcing patterns of Japanese* (RIETI Discussion paper series 12-E-027).

Baldwin, R., Kawai, M., & Wignaraya, G. (2013). *The future of the world trading system: Asian perspectives*. Tokyo: Centre for Economic Policy Research and the Asian Development Bank Institute.

Falck-Reyes, M. (2015). La respuesta de las multinacionales japonesas frente al estancamiento interno y el Nuevo entorno internacional de la fragmentación de la producción in López Villafañe, V. and Uscanga, Carlos, Coords., Japón después de ser el número uno. Del alto crecimiento al rápido envejecimiento (pp. 49–71). México: Siglo XXI Editores.

Financial Times. (2017) *fDiMarkets.com trends report: FDI from Japan to Mexico*. January 2003 to June 2017.

Head, K., & Mayer, T. (2015). *Brands in motion: How frictions shape multinational production* (CEPII Working paper no. ISSN: 1293-2574).

Head, K., & Mayer, T. (2016). *Reversal of regional trade agreements: Consequences of Brexit and Trumpit for the multinational car industry*. VOX CEPR's policy portal.

INEGI. (2015). *Data base Perfil de las empresas manufactureras de exportación*. http://www.inegi.org.mx/sistemas/bie/. Accessed 28 Aug 2017.

Interamerican Development Bank (IDB). (2013). *Japan and Latin America and the Caribbean: Building a sustainable trans-Pacific relationship*. Felipe Herrera Library.

International Organization of Motor Vehicles Manufacturers (OICA). (2015) http://www.oica.net/category/production-statistics/2015-statistics/. Accessed 21 Nov 2016.

JETRO-México. *Japón. Retos y Oportunidades de Negocios. Acuerdo de Asociación Económica México-Japón. 10 años. Comercio e Inversión*. Conference, 2015, June 25.

Juárez, P. (2017, May 5). Cada año llegan 100 empresas japonesas a México. *Milenio. Negocios*. Online version.

Kimura, F., & Ando, M. (2006). Japanese manufacturing FDI and International producton and distribution networks in East Asia. In S. Urata, C. S. Yue, & F. Kimura (Eds.), *Multinationals and economic growth in East Asia, Foreign direct investment, corporate strategies and national economic development*. London: Routledge.

Kuwayama, M. (2015). Japan-Latin America relations: Then and now. The Japan model of economic engagement: Opportunities for Latin America and the Caribbean. *Mundo Asia Pacífico* (Vol. 4, Núm. 7, Julio-Diciembre 2015).

Lakhera, M. L. (2008). *Japanese FDI flows in Asia, Perspectives and challenges*. Basingstoke: Palgrave Macmillan.

Ministry of Foreign Affairs of Japan. (2002, July). *Japan-Mexico Joint Study Group on the strengthening of bilateral economic relations*. Final report. http://www.mofa.go.jp/region/latin/mexico/relation0207/index.html. Accessed 3 Apr 2017.

Negocios ProMéxico. (2015). *The Mexican automotive industry: Leading the World*. Secretaría de México. http://www.promexico.gob.mx/documentos/revista-negocios/pdf/abr-2015.pdf. Accessed 19 June 2016.

NHTSA U.S. Department of Transportation, National Highway Traffic Safety Administration. http://www.nhtsa.gov/. Accessed 16 June 2016.

Nissan-Mexico. Official website: http://nissannews.com/es-MX/nissan/mexico. Accessed 31 May 2017.

Research Institute of Economy. Trade and Industry (RIETI). *RIETI TID-2015 Database.* http://www.rieti-tid.com/trade.php. Accessed 10 June 2016.

Secretaría de Economía and ProMéxico. (2015). *Diez años 2005–2015, Acuerdo para el Fortalecimiento de la Asociación Económica (AAE) entre México y Japón*. México.

Summary of the 46th Basic Survey on Overseas Business Activities. http://www.meti.go.jp/english/statistics/tyo/kaigaizi/pdf/h2c407je.pdf. Accessed 31 Aug 2017.

Villarreal, A., & Fergusson, Ian. (2017). *The North American Free Trade Agreement (NAFTA).* Congressional Research Service (CRS) report. http://publications.apec.org/publication-detail.php?pub_id=1863 Accessed 4 Sept 2017.

Yamashita, N. (2010). *International fragmentation of production*. The impact of outsourcing of the Japanese economy, Cheltenham: Edward Elgar.

Chapter 3
Locational Determinants of Japanese Automotive FDI in Mexico: A Spatial Analysis

Leo Guzman-Anaya

Abstract This study examines regional determinants of Japanese automotive firm location in Mexico. Specifically, the analysis is focused on automotive suppliers at a municipal level from 2000–2010. The results show that three main factors determine plant location: industrial park presence in a municipality, agglomeration of Japanese automotive firms, and proximity to a major Japanese automotive assembly plant. Under certain specifications, market size and labor quality were also significant. The findings suggest a preference from Japanese firms for agglomeration in production sites that facilitate the transition to the new host country and favor spatial and organizational integration between customer and supplier firm.

Keywords Japanese foreign direct investment · Location factors · Spatial analysis

3.1 Introduction

In the empirical and theoretical economic literature, Foreign Direct Investment (hereafter FDI) is regarded as a factor that stimulates economic growth.[1] Many governments, from both developed and developing countries believe that FDI can benefit the host nation through the "externalities" or "spillovers" associated with this type of investment. In this sense, Aitken and Harrison (1999) argue that many governments eased restrictions on FDI since the 1980s, and actively pursued to attract foreign investors by offering subsidies and tax incentives. Mexico was among these countries, gradually increasing the country's openness to free trade and

[1]Although there is no clear consensus on the topic, recent studies that have searched for "inter-industry" spillovers have found supporting results for the hypothesis linking FDI to productivity and technological enhancements in local firms. For comprehensive literature reviews see Gorg and Greenway (2003) and Guzman-Anaya (2013).

L. Guzman-Anaya (✉)
Human Resources Department, University of Guadalajara, Zapopan, Mexico
e-mail: leo.guzman8@gmail.com

M. Falck-Reyes, L. Guzman-Anaya (eds.), *Japanese Direct Investment in Mexico's Transport Equipment Sector*, New Frontiers in Regional Science: Asian Perspectives 22,
https://doi.org/10.1007/978-981-10-7718-0_3

FDI. According to Lichtensztejn (2014) restrictions to FDI have dropped during the last 40 years following OECD standards, and this drop has been more noticeable for the automotive industry where restrictions are below OECD levels and other industries in Mexico. The attraction of FDI has thus been an important government strategy for economic development in developing countries and the location determinant an important issue for policy makers.

The early work from Marshall (1920) provided three seminal arguments for spatially agglomerated industries: concentration increases the pool of skilled and specialized workers, promotes the development of specialized inputs, and facilitates the presence of technological and productivity spillovers among firms. For the case of foreign firms, Huang and Wei (2011) mention that the FDI distribution within a host country is a spatially and temporally varying process.

The choice of studying Japanese automotive suppliers and their location decisions in Mexico is motivated by several factors. First, Japanese FDI (JFDI) flows to Mexico have increased since the signing of the Mexico-Japan Economic Partnership Agreement (EPA) in 2005 and most investment has been concentrated in the automotive industry. Second, most research on FDI location factors for the case of Mexico has been conducted without taking into account the nationality of the investor, failing to identify disparities that might arise from different sources of investment. Third, previous studies on the location choices of JFDI have focused on the case of China or the U.S. with scarce information for other countries, limiting the understanding on the location factors important to JFDI. Finally, understanding the determinants of JFDI location for the case of Mexico will augment previous findings of intra-country spatial distribution of FDI and provide knowledge for policy makers that intend to influence the location distribution of Japanese investment.

3.2 JFDI in Mexico

JFDI increased worldwide during the 1980s as a result of the Plaza accord of 1985, which led to an appreciation of the Japanese Yen and loss of competitiveness of Japanese products in international markets, particularly in the United States (US). This phenomenon incited Japanese firms to locate production activities abroad and ignited research trying to explain the location decision of JFDI.

For the case of JFDI in Mexico, with the signing of the Mexico-Japan Economic Partnership Agreement (EPA) in 2005, JFDI flows to Mexico increased. Guzman-Anaya (2013) mentions that between 2003 and 2013 JFDI flows to Mexico grew at an annual average growth rate of over 20% with 70% of this investment concentrated in the automotive industry. Although the sharp increase of JFDI to Mexico is undeniable, little research has been conducted regarding the regional location determinants of this investment.

Figure 3.1 depicts the geographical distribution of Japanese automotive supplier firms across the 2457 Mexican municipalities in 2015. The figure shows presence and agglomeration of Japanese firms in the center, northeast and Tijuana region,

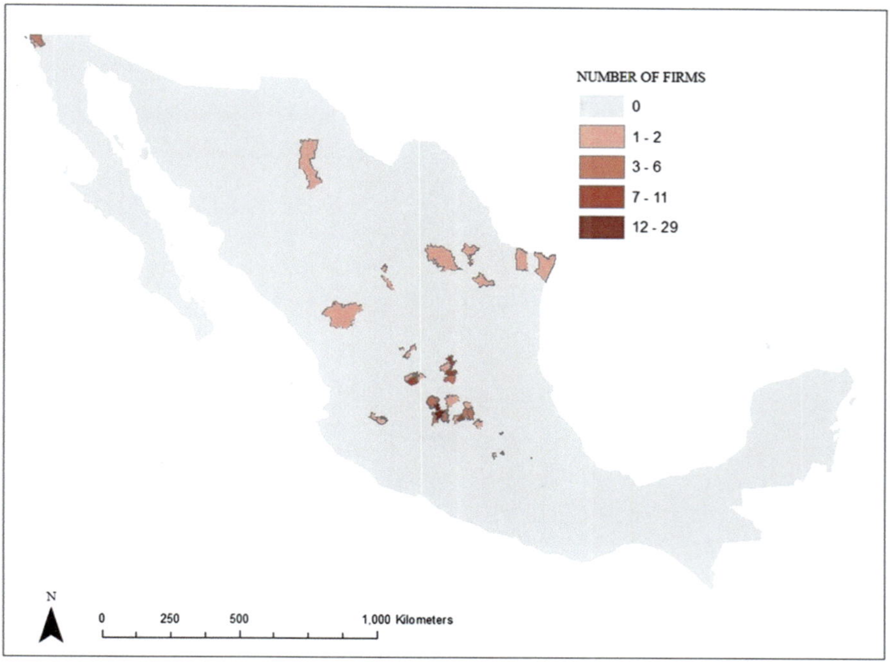

Fig. 3.1 The distribution of Japanese automotive supplier firms across Mexican municipalities, 2015 (**Source:** Author's calculations based on data from Toyo Keizai (2015/2016))

while the southern part of Mexico exhibits no presence of Japanese firms. This is to be expected, since central and northern regions in Mexico exhibit higher levels and concentration of economic development, communication and transportation infrastructure and financial and banking services, while the southern region in Mexico has been traditionally characterized by lower levels of development being not an attractive location for FDI in general.

Smith and Florida (1994) point out that an important factor in the location of Japanese suppliers in the automotive industry is the location of Japanese-affiliated automotive assemblers. There seems to be an agglomeration inclination of JFDI in the automotive industry following the organizational and production structure of their manufacturing system which favors close proximity between assemblers and suppliers of parts and components (Asanuma 1989; Aoki 1990). Belderbos and Carree (2002) argue that this becomes more evident for the case of small and medium-sized enterprises investing abroad. Figure 3.2 shows the spatial distribution of 457 Japanese automotive supplier firms and 7 Japanese automotive assemblers. From the visual representation of the data, the agglomeration of Japanese automotive firms is observed and certain spatial patterns emerge, in particular with regards to the proximity between assemblers and suppliers in the automotive industry.

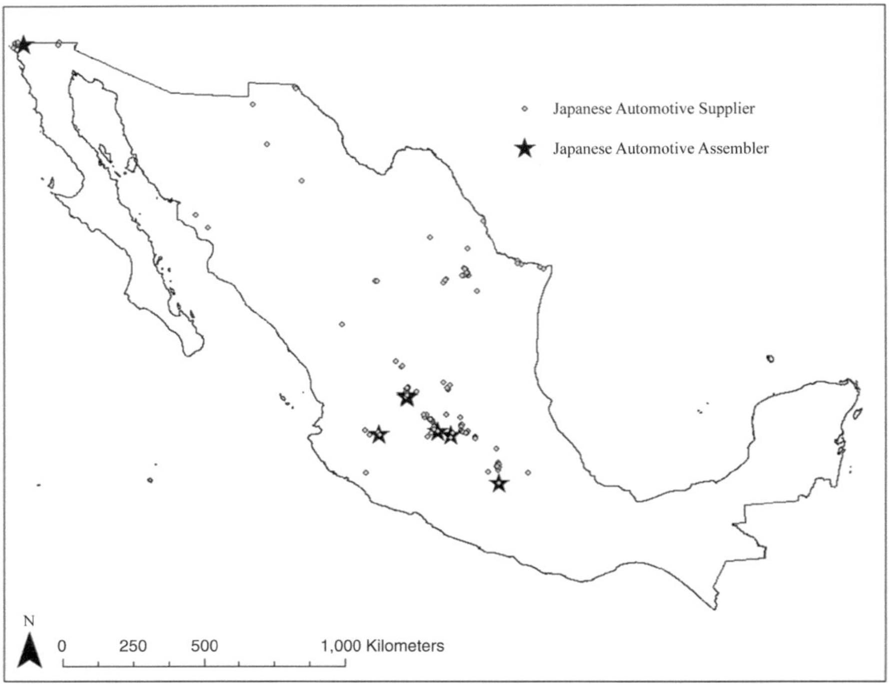

Fig. 3.2 The distribution of Japanese automotive assemblers and suppliers in Mexico, 2015 (**Source:** Author's calculations based on data from Toyo Keizai (2015/2016))

3.3 Regional Characteristics and Location Choice

3.3.1 Location Choice and FDI

The growth of FDI flows has incited extensive research on the behavior of multinational firms and the location factors associated with FDI. Little (1978) and Luger and Shetty (1985) published seminal studies focusing on spatial characteristics and determinants of FDI. The research found that higher wages deterred FDI inflows from a region, while state government spending policies affected positively the location decision of foreign firms. According to Zhou et al. (2002), empirical literature has focused on four sets of factors as determinants of FDI location: market-related factors, labor costs, infrastructure and government policies. Similarly, Jordaan (2009) mentions that regional-level factors such as regional demand, regional production costs, regional government policies and agglomeration economies influence the location decisions of multinational firms.

The literature on spatial characteristics and other determinants of the location decision of FDI has primarily focused on developed countries, while the studies focusing on developing economies is still limited. One reason for the scarcity in research for developing countries, as Cassidy and Andreosso-O'Callaghan (2006) point out, is due to the difficulty in finding or generating reliable data at a regional, municipal or state level across countries.

Most analysis on the spatial determinants of FDI in developing economies has focused on the case of China, primarily due to data availability, the surge of FDI inflows, and the uneven growth patterns caused by the special economic or export zones which in turn have aggravated regional disparities within the country (Cassidy and Andreosso-O'Callaghan 2006). Broadman and Sun (1997) found that the stock of FDI in China was determined by Gross National Product (GNP), infrastructure development, illiteracy levels and coastal location. Similarly, Chen (1997) analyzing FDI inflows to Chinese provinces found transportation infrastructure to be positively related with FDI growth in a region, while "efficiency wages" (measured by nominal wages divided by average productivity) to be negatively influencing the regional location of FDI. Huang and Wei (2011) using spatial statistics and geographically weighted regressions analyzed the spatial and temporal patterns and determinants of FDI distribution in China at the provincial level. The results show presence of spatial autocorrelation, clustering and hot spots since 2002, with the majority of local patterns of spatial autocorrelation observed in the eastern region. Also, institutional, transportation and agglomeration factors were shown to be determinants of FDI location, although these factors varied across different regions. They conclude that regional differences provide evidence that the relationship between foreign firms and local or regional environments along with transportation infrastructure play an important role in later stages of regional economic development, igniting further FDI inflows.

For the case of Mexico, previous studies have analyzed macro and regional-level factors that seem to matter in the attraction of FDI. Lichtensztejn (2014) found that FDI levels are positively related to overall Gross Domestic Product (GDP) and to openness to free trade agreements, while it is negatively linked with restrictions to FDI entrance and country-risk levels associated with crime. Similarly, Jordaan (2009) reports that state characteristics such as demand, wages, schooling, labor quality, regional distance to main markets and presence of agglomeration economies influence the location decision of new manufacturing firms. These previous studies provide an overall idea of important factors that influence the arrival of FDI in Mexico, however, they fail to analyze the location decision of a particular type of investment given by nationality which might differ not only by the type of organizational style followed by firms from different countries but also from the distance between the host and home countries. Also, taking regional or macro-level characteristics in explaining the location decisions of firms might not provide a precise insight in the location behavior of FDI, since firms have a great number of location options within the country or within a region which may be better explained at a municipal level.

3.3.2 Location Choice and JFDI

Previous empirical literature on JFDI location has provided evidence on certain factors that matter to Japanese investors; these include factors associated with regional demand, regional production costs, regional policies, regional agglomeration economies, regional infrastructure and regional strategic location.

Regional demand is believed to be a factor in FDI location. As it is noted by Chen (1997), it would be expected that larger municipal economies are more attractive to FDI projects than smaller ones, this due to the fact that larger economies create the conditions for industries and enterprises to develop via external economies of scale or spillover effects and there is more potential market demand. Cheng and Stough (2006) argue that FDI would focus on a provincial or state-level GDP rather than a national one and empirical literature usually employs GDP measures to control for market size of the municipal economy. For the case of JFDI, previous studies have shown that regional GDP has been a determinant factor for plant location in China (Belderbos and Carree 2002; Cassidy and Andreosso-O'Callaghan 2006; Cheng 2008) and the U.S. (Kotabe 1993; Woodward 1992). Zhou et al. (2002) did not find the market size variable to be significant for a study in China, which might be due to the fact that Japanese investors at the time were not focusing on local markets but trying to serve Japanese or third country markets.

For the case of regional production costs, previous studies have traditionally employed labor costs or labor quality as a way to measure production costs in a region. The cost of labor has been regarded in the literature as a key factor in explaining the location of foreign firms, especially between countries. Within a specific country, raising resource costs in a state or municipality may reveal the cost structure in neighboring locations more appealing. However, the disparities in nominal wages become less evident at the state or municipal level and conflicting results may arise when labor productivity is not included in the analysis (Coughlin and Segev 2000). In this sense, Chen (1997) suggests the use of an "efficiency wage" which incorporates the productivity of labor.[2] The study finds the efficiency wage to be negative and a statistically significant determinant of FDI. Other studies that included efficiency wages have found a positive relationship with Japanese firm location: Smith and Florida (1994), Cheng and Stough (2006) and Cheng (2008). These studies argue that Japanese firms seek a more qualified labor force that is reflected in the willingness to pay higher wages. In this sense, labor quality has also been regarded as an important factor explaining the location of JFDI. Most studies employ education measurements to reflect labor quality and usually find a positive relationship with JFDI location (Smith and Florida 1994; Cheng and Stough 2006; Cassidy and Andreosso-O'Callaghan 2006). Cheng (2008) suggests the use of the adult illiteracy rate as a proxy for labor quality and finds a negative relationship with Japanese firm location in the analysis.

The presence of integration schemes and policy incentives as a determinant of FDI location has been of interest in studies of JFDI location. The presence of good institutions exerts a positive influence on FDI location (Huang and Wei 2011). The factors pertaining to regional policies have been measured in JFDI studies in terms of presence of development zones, tax levels and state promotion policies. Studies in China have found that development zones exert a positive influence on the loca-

[2] Chen (1997) calculates the efficiency wage by dividing the average wage in a province by the average productivity per province, where the average productivity is determined by either the value-added in an industry or the industrial output by worker. Lower ratios imply higher levels of "efficiency wage" and thus a more attractive location to FDI.

tion of Japanese firms (Zhou et al. 2002; Belderbos and Carree 2002; Wakasugi 2005; Cheng and Stough 2006). On the other hand, previous studies in the U.S. find a negative relationship between Japanese firm location and the local tax rate in a state or county (Woodward 1992; Smith and Florida 1994) and mixed results with regards to state promotion policies, measured by the presence of state promotion offices in Japan (Woodward 1992; Kotabe 1993).

Due to neighboring effects, agglomeration of firms may increase the inflow of FDI to neighboring locations through the expected positive agglomeration externalities (Huang and Wei 2011). Specifically, the clustering of foreign investors may generate information externalities regarding the operating environment, access to a larger pool of specialized inputs and labor and technological spillovers (Belderbos and Carree 2002). However, Coughlin and Segev (2000) point out that if agglomeration benefits do not spill over, FDI may have negative effects on the presence of foreign firms in neighboring locations.

Coughlin et al. (1990) find that for the case of the U.S., states with higher densities of manufacturing activity were more attractive for the location of FDI. This has also been observed for the case of JFDI. Wakasugi (2005) mentions that Japanese firms abroad constitute a vertical fragmentation type of their manufacturing process, where affiliates are established abroad for the purpose of expanding the development of the parts-assembly network from the home country. In this sense, once a firm from the network plans an investment abroad, other firms follow and move production to the new host country. Moreover, the main source of information on the foreign market for Japanese firms is generally other Japanese affiliates, facilitating and encouraging the agglomeration of JFDI.[3] Also, the national preferences for amenities, i.e. schools and restaurants, proximity advantages due to the use of just-in-time delivery and inventory control systems and the demand for specialized inputs developed by long-term supplier-client relationships in Japan are attributed for the clustering choice of JFDI (Reid 1995; Head et al. 1995).

Cheng and Stough (2006) employ provincial location quotients of JFDI as an indicator of Japanese nationality agglomeration. Also, non-nationality agglomeration was measured by the number of domestic industrial enterprises for each province. Belderbos and Carree (2002) employ three different sets of agglomeration: industry agglomeration (number of establishment in a specific industry), Japanese firm agglomeration (count of existing Japanese firms in a region) and Keiretsu agglomeration (number of existing establishments in a region owned by a "core" firm or other member firms of the same vertical business group). Smith and Florida (1994) capture the effect of agglomeration by a straight-line distance between the location of a county with presence of Japanese firms to the nearest Japanese automotive assembly plant. Zhou et al. (2002) capture agglomeration by the cumulative count of Japanese subsidiaries during a previous year in a given city. The agglomeration hypothesis usually turns out statistically significant results and seems to be a determinant factor for JFDI location.

---

[3]This type of behavior by Japanese firms was observed and documented for Mexico's western region. See Kakihara and Guzman-Anaya (2014).

With regards to regional infrastructure, the literature has considered transportation infrastructure as a determinant of foreign firm location. Specifically, higher and more extensive levels of transportation infrastructure are associated with higher levels of JFDI. This has been confirmed by Chen (1997), Coughlin and Segev (2000) for the case of China. Also, Cassidy and Andreosso-O'Callaghan (2006) suggests that the transportation function for China should be divided into three key infrastructures: highways, railways and waterways. Cheng and Stough (2006) suggest the use of a density indicator of infrastructure, which is represented by the ratio between a region's infrastructure capacities to its geographic size. In this sense, Wakasugi (2005) employs a transportation network index, measured as total length of roads, railways and inland sea routes per square kilometer in a region. Belderbos and Carree (2002) include dummy variables to control for sea ports in a region and a measure of telecommunication infrastructure quality measured by the number of long-distance telephone lines per capita. Also, urbanization levels have been used as proxies for regional infrastructure. Specifically, population density has been shown to be a positive factor in attracting JFDI (Woodward 1992; Smith and Florida 1994).

Regional strategic location has also been employed in previous studies that explain Japanese firm location choice. For the case of China, Cassidy and Andreosso-O'Callaghan (2006) point out that the importance of geographical location lies in the adjacency to port facilities that facilitate trade and easy access to ships. Also, the government policies that promoted the creation of "Special Economic Zones" and later "Economic and Technological Development Zones" incentivized the location of foreign firms in coastal cities along the eastern seaboard. Similar results are reported by Huang and Wei (2011), where the concentration of FDI in eastern China is further explained by a multi-scalar spatial-temporal analysis that shows certain regional characteristics such as institutional, transportation and agglomeration factors as determinants of this particular concentration of investment. Belderbos and Carree (2002) employ a variable representing the distance from Japan to the host country measured by flight hours from Tokyo to the region's main airport; they argue that controlling and managing overseas affiliates, and communication and transportation costs increase with distance and a negative relationship is explained. The strategic location of a state, county or municipality has been explored in different areas, for example: in terms of distance to Japan (Belderbos and Carree 2002), trade activity (Zhou et al. 2002), area size of the state/county (Woodward 1992; Zhou et al. 2002; Cheng 2008), climate (Woodward 1992), bordering state activity (Head et al. 1995), life quality (Woodward 1992) and presence of minority population (Woodward 1992; Smith and Florida 1994).

3.3.3 Location Choice and Automotive JFDI

Previous literature on location factors of JFDI in the automotive industry has shed some interesting results. Mair et al. (1988) researched the transplant of automobile complexes and manufacturing plants in North America; specifically, the location of

250 components and parts firms and 12 assembly plants. Mair et al. (1988) mention that the main concern for location selection of JFDI was the implementation of just-in-time manufacturing techniques, where a trade-off between greenfield sites with a more amenable workforce and proximity between supplier and assembly firms existed. Suppliers concentrated within one to 2 h driving distance to the assembly plant but also dispersed at the local scale to avoid labor market overlaps. Finally, the results point out that subsidies offered by provincial, state or local governments to attract JFDI had little or no impact on the overall geographical distribution of Japanese automotive investment.

Hyun (2008) analyzed JFDI in the European automotive industry during the 1980s. The change in the mode of market entry from exports to establishing production facilities was to allegedly circumvent existing or expected trade barriers, reduce financial constraints generated by an appreciating yen and trim increasing trade frictions that accused Japan of not granting sufficient market access to European market imports.[4] In this context Hyun (2008) considered JFDI as trade-substituting FDI searching to maintain existing market share or to avoid diverted trade flows. Automotive JFDI in Europe concentrated in the U.K. with major projects from Nissan, Honda and Toyota. Compared to the U.K., other European countries showed considerable disparities where most of the investment came in the form of joint ventures at a much lower scale.

Wakasugi (2005) analyzed the location choices of automotive FDI in China during the 1990s. The study found that JFDI projects were drawn to specific areas depending on the agglomeration of other Japanese firms and the existence of special economic zones. Interestingly, the results showed that the transportation equipment industry follows its own industry-specific factors compared with other industries. Head et al. (1995) finds that the keiretsu agglomeration effect in the location decision from JFDI is primarily present in activities related with the automotive industry. Similarly, Smith and Florida (1994) report that a determinant factor for the location decision of automotive JFDI in the U.S. is the presence of Japanese-affiliated automotive assemblers. Also, the study shows that Japanese firms prefer locations with large populations, high manufacturing density and higher wages. The location of Japanese firms in communities that exhibit higher wages is explained by a preference for higher quality human resources and greater labor force stability. Similar results for the U.S. are reported by Graham and Krugman (1989). Woodward (1992) mentions that JFDI in the automotive industry avoids counties with high African-American population densities, areas with high unemployment and greenfield investment sites, but are drawn to locations with presence of interstate highways.

[4] Hyun (2008) mentions two main policies that the European community put forward to hinder Japanese companies' market access. First, a strict reciprocity guarantee from Japan to create mutual balance of advantages and increase the position of European car manufacturers. And second, a Voluntary Export Restraint (VER) on Japanese cars limiting the market share obtained in Europe until European car manufacturers reached similar levels in Japanese markets.

3.4 Methodology

3.4.1 Data Sources

The present analysis uses disaggregated firm-level JFDI data from the *Kaigai Shinshutsu Kigyou Souran-Kuni Betsu* (Japanese Overseas Investments – by country) a publication of Toyo Keizai. Toyo Keizai conducts an annual survey of overseas activities from Japanese firms all over the world and for the purpose of this study data was gathered from the 2014 and 2015 directories[5] (Toyo Keizai Inc. 2014/2015). The 2014 and 2015 editions of the directory listed a total of 457 firms in Mexico, in which location and industrial activity was specified.[6] From the initial database, a total of 244 firms were selected pertaining to their activities in the automotive industry.

According to Yamawaki (1991), the Toyo Keizai publication lists virtually the total population of Japanese foreign subsidiaries by host country. Also, the Toyo Keizai directory has been widely employed in previous studies investigating JFDI location choices (Head et al. 1995; Zhou et al. 2002; Belderbos and Carree 2002; Wakasugi 2005; Cassidy and Andreosso-O'Callaghan 2006; Cheng and Stough 2006; Cheng 2008).

Data on the municipal characteristics in Mexico was gathered from three sources: *Sistema Estatal y Municipal de Bases de Datos* from the National Institute of Statistics and Geography (Mexico's national statistical office), a large compendium of state and municipal level statistics (INEGI 2016). Also, from the *Índice de Desarrollo Municipal* (municipal level human development statistics) published by the United Nations Development Program (UNDP 2016). The third source was from statistics published from *Consejo Nacional de Evaluación de la Política de Desarrollo Social* (The national council for social development policy evaluation). The data was obtained for three time periods: 2000, 2005 and 2010 (CONEVAL 2016).

Based on the subsidiary records and further analysis, the exact firm location was pinned using geographical coordinates and Geographical Information System (GIS) software; this allowed for agglomeration of the data at a municipal level. Also, the year of establishment was identified and due to the data structure of the independent variables, Japanese automotive firm counts of new establishments at the municipal level were compiled at three data points (2000, 2005 and 2010). A total of 61 municipalities received at least one Japanese firm during the period of analysis. With 2457 municipalities, and three time periods, the data set exhibited 7371 observations.

---

[5] The directory compiles information on the overseas activities of Japanese firms all over the world.

[6] It is important to point out that for some firms only state-level location was specified, so additional research to determine the specific municipal-level location was conducted. Also, some observations did not specify the industrial activity of the firm. For these cases further information was gathered through the company's website or from Japan's Chamber of Commerce and Industry Directory 2015. This directory is published at an annual basis. It includes information on the activities of Japanese firms in Mexico, including: company name, address, contact information (telephone, fax, and email), website and industrial activity (www.japon.org.mx).

3.4.2 Variables

The independent variable, JAP_{it}, reflects the presence of JFDI activity in municipality *i* in time period *t*, and is measured by the total number of new Japanese subsidiary firms. For a given period, if there was no arrival of Japanese firms in a given municipality, a zero would be recorded. From the total of 7371 municipality-year combinations, there were 7285 cases with zero records of JAP_{it}.

From the previous literature on the location factors of JFDI in a host country, six regional determinants were identified as important to Japanese firms. These included: regional demand, regional production costs, regional policies, regional agglomeration economies, regional infrastructure and regional strategic location. This study will attempt to test if these determinants are significant for Japanese automotive plant location in Mexico.

To capture the effect of regional demand, municipal level GDP is included as a proxy for market size in a municipality; the expected relationship is positive in explaining JFDI location.

Regional production costs were controlled for via the municipal level illiteracy rate. Since there is willingness from Japanese firms to pay higher wages and thus employ a more educated workforce, a negative sign is expected.

For this research, it was not possible to find disaggregated data on any of the proxies used by previous studies to reflect regional policies at the municipal level; therefore, a dummy variable was constructed to reflect the presence of industrial parks in a given municipality, the variable was coded as 1 if, in time period *t*, the municipality had an industrial park, and 0 otherwise. This proxy aims to reflect the presence of development policies seeking to attract FDI in a region. A positive coefficient sign is expected.

To account for the presence of regional agglomeration economies, a variable was constructed measuring the cumulative count of Japanese automotive subsidiaries in a municipality in *t-1*. The variable intends to measure the regional agglomeration of JFDI and its effects on new firm arrival. A positive effect on the dependent variable is anticipated.

The presence of regional infrastructure is usually accounted for in previous studies via transportation infrastructure or urbanization in a region. For this study, the urbanization proxy is used to explore the relationship between infrastructure and Japanese firm location. The variable is measured as total population in a municipality in time *t*. A positive sign is hypothesized.

Finally, the strategic location of a municipality might influence the decision of plant location for Japanese investors. For the case of Japanese automotive suppliers, it has been shown that new plant location is dependent on the proximity to Japanese automotive assemblers. Therefore, to proxy for the regional strategic location of a municipality, calculations were carried out to first determine the centroid of each municipality and afterwards conduct linear measurements to the closest Japanese automotive assembler. Each municipality had a unique record of distance to the closest assembler. A negative relationship between the distance variable and Japanese firm location is expected.

3.4.3 Econometric Model

Studies that analyze the location choice of foreign firms have traditionally employed conditional logit estimation techniques to examine how regional factors affect the location decision of FDI. This has also been the case for studies investigating Japanese firms (Woodward 1992; Head et al. 1995; Belderbos and Carree 2002; Wakasugi 2005; Cheng and Stough 2006). However, Cheng (2008) suggests that the conditional/multinomial logit model suffers from certain limitations and recommends the use of the mixed logit model to overcome the rigid proportionate substitution pattern found in earlier models. The study advances the use of discrete choice models to examine Japanese investors' decisions.

Cassidy and Andreosso-O'Callaghan (2006) suggest the use of cross-sectional OLS with a heteroskedasticity consistent covariance matrix for studies using cross-sectional data. Other studies of JFDI location choice have used the Tobit estimation technique to handle the presence of a censored dependent variable and deal with the issue of truncated data at higher or lower values with zero counts in most locations analyzed (Smith and Florida 1994; Zhou et al. 2002). Also, Zhou et al. (2002) suggest the Negative Binomial model as a suitable estimation technique when analyzing data with count outcomes.

For this analysis, due to the data structure employed, with truncated data at lower values and count outcomes, the models proposed for the econometric estimation are the Tobit and Negative Binomial models.

Also, since the earlier studies on foreign firm location determinants, advances on the estimation techniques have been developed. Recent studies on FDI location factors include a spatial component in the analysis. Moran's I index is commonly used to confirm spatial dependence; it reveals spatial agglomeration by analyzing spatial autocorrelation among regions (Anselin 1988). However, Moran's I evaluates the global dependence or clustering tendency in all regions, and it is not able to detect the presence of local cluster patterns. To assess local spatial clustering around an individual location, the Local Indicator of Spatial Association (LISA) may confirm spatial dependence for each region in the data (Anselin 1995). This study uses both Moran's I and LISA statistics to evaluate the presence of spatial dependence in the data.

If a spatial dependence is confirmed in the data, it is necessary to specify a model that captures this dependence; failing to do so will produce a specification error due to variable omission (Romero and Andres-Rosales 2014). For the case of FDI location analysis, there are reasons to suspect spatial dependence. Blanc-Brude et al. (2014) argue that ignoring a spatial dependence will generate econometric problems in FDI analysis because each observation will be partly predictable from the observations in neighboring locations.

Given the data structure employed in the study, it seems necessary to account for a panel and a spatial effect. The random effects or fixed effects panel models may be extended by introducing a spatial weights matrix (W) composed of elements (w_{ij}) that account for spatial dependence between municipality i and j. The matrix reflects the strength of dependence between municipalities. For this study, the measure of distance is assumed in terms of geographical distance, using a queen-type contiguity measure where a 1 is recorded if two municipalities share common border and 0 otherwise.

Blanc-Brude et al. (2014) mention that spatial dependence may be controlled for by introducing a spatially lagged dependent variable (SAR model), a spatially correlated error term (SEM model), or both (SEM-SAR model). Also, it is possible to include average-neighbor values of the independent variables to the specification, what is known in the literature as the Spatial Durbin model (SD model). The spatial autoregressive parameter (ρ) in the SAR model captures the spatial effect of neighboring municipalities' Japanese firm presence on the arrival of JFDI in municipality i. The spatially-correlated error term (λ) points out possible measurement errors and spatial influence through the error terms. The Spatial Durbin model includes a term (θ) which captures the independent variable effects of neighboring municipalities on municipality i. It is also possible to allow for serial correlation in the time-series errors via a serial correlation parameter (φ) giving a variety of potential spatial regression models.

3.5 Estimation Results

The starting point in the analysis was to estimate the Tobit and Negative Binomial models. Table 3.1 reports seven models, developed in a hierarchical manner under the Tobit procedure. Model fit statistics show that the inclusion of additional variables across models improved the estimation results significantly. In model 1, land area was the sole variable. Under this specification, the assumption is that JFDI location is a random decision, where larger municipalities will receive larger amounts of investment (Zhou et al. 2002; Cheng 2008). In model 2, market size was included to capture the effect of municipal level GDP on the location of Japanese firms. Model 3 included the labor quality variable, measured by the illiteracy rate. Model 4 adds the population by municipality as a proxy for urbanization. Model 5 incorporates the dummy variable reflecting the presence of industrial parks in a municipality. The agglomeration variable was included in model 6 to capture the attraction effect of prior Japanese automotive subsidiary establishment. Finally, distance to the closest Japanese automotive assembler was added in model 7 to reflect the strategic location of each municipality.

Analyzing the variables of interest, the expected signs are reported in the results. The land area variable is statistically significant only in model 1 and marginally significant in model 7. This reflects that the location of Japanese automotive assemblers is not a random decision and depends on municipal characteristics. The market size variable is positive and statistically significant in all specifications, showing the importance of economic activity in a region as a factor for Japanese firm location. These results are consistent with prior research on JFDI location (Kotabe 1993; Woodward 1992; Belderbos and Carree 2002; Cassidy and Andreosso-O'Callaghan 2006; Cheng 2008).

Table 3.1 Tobit model estimation results

TOBIT estimation							
Variables	Model 1	Model 2	Model 3	Model 4	Model 5	Model 6	Model 7
1. Land area	1.189*** (4.47)	0.193 (0.80)	0.243 (1.00)	0.261 (1.06)	−0.094 (−0.39)	−0.038 (−0.17)	0.446* (1.76)
2. Market size		2.941*** (9.03)	2.798*** (8.62)	3.229*** (2.82)	2.249** (2.03)	1.935* (1.89)	2.283** (2.16)
3. Labor quality			−0.034* (−1.74)	−0.033* (−1.66)	−0.025 (−1.34)	−0.037** (−2.10)	−0.042** (−2.39)
4. Urbanization				−0.534 (−0.40)	−0.582 (−0.44)	−0.566 (−0.44)	−1.305 (−1.03)
5. Industrial park					7.634*** (7.56)	6.294*** (6.72)	6.059*** (6.76)
6. JFDI agglomeration						1.566*** (5.12)	1.338*** (4.58)
7. Distance							−1.265** (−4.36)
Intercept	−43.762*** (−6.89)	−78.886*** (−8.53)	−75.793*** (−8.25)	−79.066*** (−6.30)	−52.118*** (−4.63)	−45.604*** (−4.42)	−38.311*** (−3.71)
N	7371	7328	7328	7242	7242	7242	7242
Log likelihood	−636.31	−508.73	−507.17	−507.096	−465.174	−451.137	−450.930
Incremental chi-square	–	254.14***	3.12***	0.16***	83.85***	28.07***	20.41***
Noncensored cases	86	86	86	86	86	86	86

Note: ***p<0.01, **p<0.05, *p<0.10
Figures in parentheses express t-statistics

The regional production costs hypothesis is confirmed by the results. Japanese automotive firms seem to establish in locations that reflect higher levels of labor quality. This is shown by the negative relationship between firm location and the municipal illiteracy rate and confirms previous results from Cheng (2008).

Interestingly, the urbanization variable did not turn out statistical significant coefficients. The results seem to reflect no real preference from JFDI for locations with populous areas; in other words, Japanese firms might locate in municipalities that provide a more numerous labor pool and higher degree of urbanization, but might as well establish in rural, greenfield locations.

The presence of industrial parks, reflecting regional level development policies seeking to attract FDI, turned out to be one of the determinant factors for Japanese firm location. The coefficients were positive and highly significant in the models that included this variable. The results suggest that Japanese firms seek for locations with an adequate investment environment reflected by the presence of FDI policies designated to develop production infrastructure that facilitates the arrival of foreign firms to Mexico.

Similarly, another determinant factor found in the results is the presence of Japanese firm agglomeration. The results show that municipalities that attract Japanese firms become highly sought after by future Japanese firms investing in the automotive industry. This might be the result of positive externalities been generated by the agglomeration of economic activity and also by the fact that competing Japanese firms share and value information regarding possible investment locations (Kakihara and Guzman-Anaya 2014). These results confirm previous findings that show the propensity of Japanese investment to cluster spatially in the host country (Head et al. 1995; Belderbos and Carree 2002; Zhou et al. 2002; Wakasugi 2005; Cheng and Stough 2006; Cheng 2008).

Finally, the distance variable turned out negative and statistically significant. The results suggest that the presence of Japanese assembly plants is an important element in the location decision of Japanese automotive suppliers. Once Japanese firms locate in Mexico, they seem to locate in clustered production sites where a pulling factor is the establishment of automotive assemblers. Smith and Florida (1994) mention that this type of production preference helps Japanese firms capitalize on lower transaction costs and enables the presence of technological, information and productivity spillovers facilitating the spatial and organizational integration between customer and supplier firms.

To examine the robustness of the reported coefficients, all model specifications were estimated using the Negative Binomial model (see Table 3.2). The results remained consistent for the three determinant variables of JFDI location (industrial park presence, JFDI agglomeration and distance to Japanese assembly plant). Also, urbanization remained with no explanatory power as in the previous models. Similarly, the land area variable behaved as in the Tobit model. The market size variable was positive and statistically significant in specifications 9, 10 and 14. The labor quality variable was significant only in model 14.

From previous empirical findings, there are reasons to suspect the presence of spatial dependence in FDI models, especially at the regional level. First, the Moran's

Table 3.2 Negative binomial model estimation results

Negative binomial estimation							
Variables	Model 8	Model 9	Model 10	Model 11	Model 12	Model 13	Model 14
1. Land area	0.505*** (4.40)	−0.097 (−0.85)	−0.093 (−0.81)	−0.116 (−0.99)	−0.103 (−0.99)	−0.046 (−0.47)	0.258** (2.31)
2. Market size		1.134*** (11.07)	1.121*** (10.66)	0.566 (1.35)	0.444 (1.13)	0.321 (0.86)	0.687* (1.66)
3. Labor quality			−0.004 (−0.62)	−0.066 (−0.95)	−0.004 (−0.63)	−0.010 (−1.53)	−0.016** (−2.29)
4. Urbanization				0.681 (1.34)	0.381 (0.78)	0.456 (0.98)	−0.174 (−0.34)
5. Industrial park					3.245*** (10.82)	2.659*** (8.68)	2.604*** (8.45)
6. JFDI agglomeration						0.579*** (2.94)	0.483*** (2.63)
7. Distance							−0.808*** (−6.13)
Intercept	−13.408*** (−5.96)	−24.273*** (−9.79)	−23.917*** (−9.39)	−19.640*** (−4.91)	−15.333*** (−3.91)	−14.581*** (−3.98)	−11.437*** (−2.87)
N	7371	7328	7328	7328	7328	7328	7328
Log likelihood	−602.964	−505.05	−504.855	−503.962	−445.867	−437.753	−416.629
Incremental chi-square	–	214.24***	0.40***	1.78***	116.19***	16.23***	42.25***

Note: ***p<0.01, **p<0.05, *p<0.10
Figures in parentheses express z-statistics

I statistic was calculated to detect spatial dependence in the dependent variable. Table 3.3 shows the results for the 2000, 2005 and 2010 periods. The results show no presence of spatial dependence in the data; however, the Moran's I statistic is not able to detect presence of local cluster patterns. From the data analyzed, it seems that Japanese firms follow certain spatial clustering around a specific location; therefore the LISA statistic was also computed to search for spatial dependence.

Figures 3.3, 3.4 and 3.5 show the LISA cluster map for the years 2000, 2005 and 2010 respectively. For the year 2000, the results indicate local clustering of the low-low type for 678 cases, meaning that these municipalities fail to attract JFDI and this "unattractiveness" spills over to neighboring municipalities. Four municipalities exhibit a high-high type of clustering, explained by high values of Japanese firm presence that spills over to nearby municipalities (with high values as well). Also, there are 102 cases with a low-high and 23 cases with a high-low type of spatial outlier also referred to as negative spatial autocorrelation. The map for the 2005 values indicates 1845 cases with a low-low type of clustering, 1 case with a high-high type of clustering, 61 cases with a low-high type of spatial outlier and 12 cases

Table 3.3 Moran's I statistic for spatial autocorrelation, 2000, 2005 and 2010

	2000		2005		2010	
	Moran's I	p-value	Moran's I	p-value	Moran's I	p-value
JAP	0.014	0.079	0.004	0.146	0.004	0.138

Source: Author's calculations

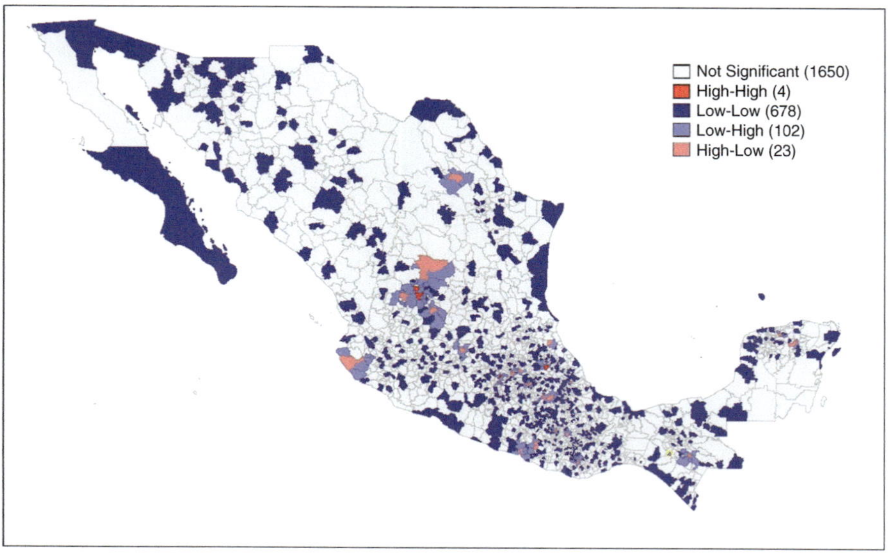

Fig. 3.3 LISA Cluster map 2000 (**Source:** Author's calculations based on data from Toyo Keizai (2015/2016))

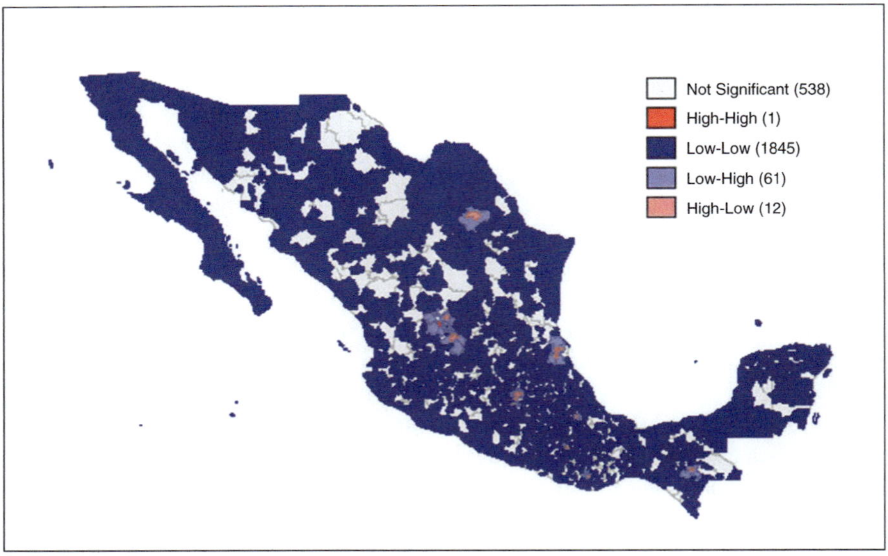

Fig. 3.4 LISA Cluster map 2005 (**Source:** Author's calculations based on data from Toyo Keizai (2015/2016))

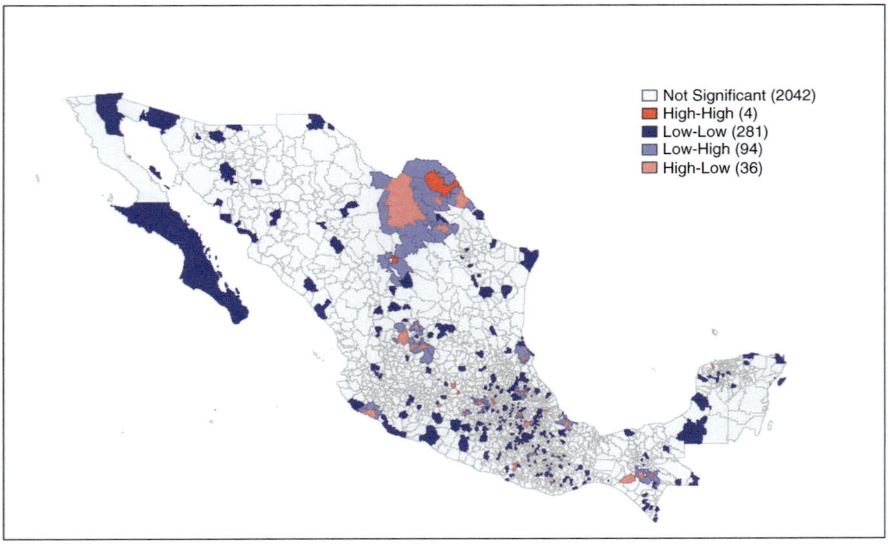

Fig. 3.5 LISA Cluster map 2010 (**Source:** Author's calculations based on data from Toyo Keizai (2015/2016))

Table 3.4 SAR and SD model estimation results

	Model 15	Model 16	
Variables	SAR	SD	θ
1. Land area	−0.042** (−2.50)	0.005 (0.98)	−0.001 (−0.18)
2. Market size	−0.004 (−0.58)	0.001 (0.18)	−0.001 (−0.59)
3. Labor quality	−0.0001 (−0.10)	0.004 (0.98)	−0.0001 (−0.68)
4. Urbanization	0.001 (0.14)	0.004 (0.43)	−0.001 (−0.41)
5. Industrial park	0.474*** (10.43)	0.447*** (11.06)	−0.124*** (−7.59)
6. JFDI agglomeration	0.503*** (17.63)	0.559*** (22.22)	−0.183*** (−18.89)
7. Distance	−0.030*** (−4.65)	−0.048*** (−5.34)	0.006*** (3.04)
Intercept	0.666*** (4.65)	0.410*** (3.09)	
ρ	0.2999***	0.2999***	
N	7371	7371	
Log likelihood	−7877.17	−7599.68	

Note: ***p<0.01, **p<0.05, *p<0.10
Figures in parentheses express t-statistics

with a high-low type of spatial outlier. Finally, for the year 2010, the data showed high-high and low-low type of spatial clustering in 281 and 4 cases respectively. On the other hand, there was a low-high and high-low type of spatial outlier in 94 and 36 cases accordingly.

The results shown by the LISA statistics suggest a spatial autocorrelation that needs to be controlled for in the econometric estimation. However, before estimating the spatial panel models, a "non-spatial" Fixed Effects (FE) and Random Effects (RE) models were evaluated.[7] The FE model performed poorly, the F-test failed to reject the hypothesis that all the coefficients in the model were different than zero; this might be due to the data structure employed, with only three time periods and 2457 municipalities. On the other hand, the RE model performed much better, the estimation was statistically significant explaining 15% of the variation in the dependent variable. Also, the industrial park, JFDI agglomeration and distance variables were all statistically significant (p<0.01).

After a visual representation of the dependent variable, the results from the Moran's I, the LISA statistics and exploratory panel models, there are reasons to suspect the presence of a spatial component in data; therefore two spatial panel regression models were estimated: the SAR model and SD model, both under random effects specifications. Results are presented in Table 3.4.

The coefficient estimates for the explanatory variables under the SAR model and SD model remain consistent under both specifications and close to the results for the non-spatial RE model, signaling a lack of omitted variable bias in the original specifications (Blanc-Brude et al. 2014). The results show that the presence of industrial parks and JFDI agglomeration have positive effects explaining Japanese firm location, while distance to a Japanese assembly plant exhibits the expected negative relationship. This confirms the findings presented in previous models. The spatial

[7] The results from these regressions are not reported, but are available upon request.

autocorrelation coefficient is strong (0.299) in both the SAR and SD model signaling spatial dependence in the model. Also, the SD model illustrates spatial effects of neighboring municipalities on the location of Japanese firms. Specifically, the variables controlling for industrial park presence, JFDI agglomeration in a municipality and distance to an assembly plant all have neighboring effects. In other words, there is a spatial effect from a municipality that exhibits these characteristics with regards to the location of Japanese automotive firms in neighboring municipalities.

Finally, there are no traditional R^2 measures of goodness-of-fit for spatial models (Anselin 1988). However, as Blanc-Brude et al. (2014) mention, since the models are estimated using maximum likelihood, the Akaike Information Criterion (AIC) may be used to compare the relative goodness-of-fit among competing models. The AIC is calculated as twice the absolute value of the log-likelihood plus twice the number of model parameters and the model with the lowest AIC results in the best fitting model. The results from the calculations indicated an AIC value of 15,768 for the SAR model and 15,213 for the SD model, suggesting a better fit of the SD model for the data.

3.6 Conclusions

Mexico is one of the largest recipients of FDI flows in the developing world. This was achieved due to active trade promotion and economic liberalization policies that began in the late 1980s. During that time, as Jordaan (2009) mentions, important spatial readjustments of economic activity in Mexico were observed. Specifically, states that share a border with the U.S. rapidly developed and there was a regional distribution of economic activity with a limited number of regional production centers in the north and center of the country. Previous results on FDI location in Mexico seem to indicate that investment tends to gravitate and agglomerate within these regional production centers.

Also, since the signing of the EPA, JFDI presence in Mexico increased with a clear concentration in the automotive industry. However, there is still scarce information explaining the factors that determined the location decisions within the country. Using georeferencing tools for Japanese automotive assembly plants and automotive supplier firms in Mexico, agglomeration patterns emerged in the center, northeast and Tijuana regions. Also, from the visual representation of the data, spatial clustering was detected, showing close proximity between assemblers and suppliers in the automotive industry.

Previous findings indicated that certain regional determinants influence the location decision of JFDI. The six regional determinants tested in this analysis were: regional demand, regional production costs, regional policies, regional agglomeration economies, regional infrastructure and regional strategic location.

Based on the estimation results from the Tobit and Negative Binomial models, the analysis produced important empirical findings. First, looking at the Tobit model specifications, the evidence suggests that regional characteristics such as market size and labor quality influence the location of Japanese automotive suppliers. Furthermore, the findings also indicate that the presence of industrial parks, JFDI agglomeration and proximity to a Japanese automotive assembly plant play an important role. Interestingly, the urbanization variable did not carry a significant coefficient, indicating that Japanese firms may locate in municipalities with higher levels of urbanization, or in rural, greenfield locations.

Second, from the Negative Binomial model the results remained consistent for the three determinant variables of JFDI location: industrial park presence, JFDI agglomeration and proximity to a Japanese assembly plant. Also, urbanization remained with no explanatory power as in the previous models.

Third, after a visual representation of the data and based on previous empirical findings, there were reasons to suspect the presence of spatial dependence in the models at a regional level. Therefore, the Moran's I statistic and LISA statistic were computed to search for spatial dependence in the dependent variable. The results indicated no presence of spatial dependence in the data at an aggregated level but did confirm the presence of local cluster patterns. The LISA statistics indicated a spatial autocorrelation that needed to be controlled for in the econometric estimations.

Fourth, after estimating a FE and RE model, the results suggested the use of spatial panel regression techniques under the SAR and SD models with random effects. The coefficient estimates remained consistent for the main variables explaining Japanese firm location. The presence of industrial parks as a proxy for regional policies that seek to attract FDI remained as one of the determinant factors in JFDI location. This result suggests that Japanese automotive suppliers seek for locations with policies that generate a favorable investment environment and productive infrastructure that eases the establishment of the firm in host country. Also, the agglomeration of Japanese automotive firms resulted in a determinant factor of new Japanese firm arrival. This is not surprising for the case of Japanese firms, where it has been shown that investors value locations with presence of other Japanese firms in vertically or horizontally related industries (Head et al. 1995; Belderbos and Carree 2002; Zhou et al. 2002; Wakasugi 2005; Cheng and Stough 2006; Cheng 2008; Kakihara and Guzman-Anaya 2014). The final factor that was consistent across different estimation techniques was the distance to a major automotive assembly plant. The findings give reason to believe that Japanese automotive suppliers gravitate towards locations in close proximity to Japanese assembly plants. Therefore, Japanese firms that establish in Mexico, locate in clustered production sites where a pulling factor is the establishment of automotive assemblers, similar to the results reported for by Smith and Florida (1994) for the U.S.

Finally, this study has shown that Japanese firms investing abroad search for locations with specific characteristics. It is clear from the results that Japanese automotive suppliers agglomerate in production clusters that facilitate the spatial and organizational integration between customer and supplier firms. This type of production preference allows Japanese firms to capitalize on lower transaction costs, creates economies of scales and fosters cooperation, providing an environment for the transfer of technology and business relations between companies at a local, national and international level. In this sense, the presence of production clusters seems to enable the presence of positive externalities in the form of technological, information and productivity spillovers. However, future research should demonstrate the presence of intra and inter-industry benefits to foreign and local firms due to JFDI presence at a disaggregated level incorporating the spatial dimension in the analysis.

References

Aitken, B., & Harrison, A. (1999). Do domestic firms benefit from foreign direct investment? Evidence from Venezuela. *American Economic Review, 89*(3), 605–618.

Anselin, L. (1988). *Spatial econometrics: Methods and models*. Boston: Kluwer Academic Publishers.

Anselin, L. (1995). Local indicators of spatial association. *Geographical Analysis, 27*(2), 93–115.

Aoki, M. (1990). Toward and economic model of the Japanese firm. *Journal of Economic Literature, 28*(1), 1–27.

Asanuma, B. (1989). Manufacturer-supplier relationships in Japan and the concept of relation specific skill. *Journal of the Japanese and International Economies, 3*(1), 1–30.

Belderbos, R., & Carree, M. (2002). The location of Japanese investment in China: Agglomeration effects, Keiretsu and firm heterogeneity. *Journal of the Japanese and International Economies, 16*(2), 194–211.

Blanc-Brude, F., Cookson, G., Piesse, J., & Strange, R. (2014). The FDI location decision: Distance and the effects of spatial dependence. *International Business Review, 23*(4), 797–810.

Broadman, H. G., & Sun, X. (1997). The distribution of foreign direct investment in China. *The World Economy, 20*(3), 339–361.

Cassidy, J. F., & Andreosso-O'Callaghan, B. (2006). Spatial determinants of Japanese FDI in China. *Japan and the World Economy, 18*(4), 512–527.

Chen, C. (1997). *Provincial characteristics and foreign direct investment location decision in China* (University of Adelaide, Chinese Economic Research Unit Working Paper, No. 97/16).

Cheng, S. (2008). Location decision variations of Japanese investors in China. *The Review of Regional Studies, 38*(3), 395–415.

Cheng, S., & Stough, R. R. (2006). Location decisions of Japanese new manufacturing plants in China: A discrete-choice analysis. *The Annals of Regional Science, 40*(2), 369–387.

CONEVAL. (2016). Consejo Nacional de Evaluación de la Política de Desarrollo Social. www.coneval.org.mx. Accessed 02 Mar 2016.

Coughlin, C., & Segev, E. (2000). Foreign direct investment in China: A spatial econometric study. *World Economy, 23*(1), 1–23.

Coughlin, C., Terza, J. V., & Arromdee, V. (1990). State government effects on the location of foreign direct investment. *Regional Science Perspectives, 20*(1), 194–207.

Gorg, H., & Greenway, D. (2003). Much Ado about nothing? Do domestic firms really benefit from foreign direct investment. *The World Bank Research Observer, 19*(2), 171–197.

Graham, E. M., & Krugman, P. R. (1989). *Foreign direct investment in the United States*. Washington, DC: Institute for International Economics.

Guzman-Anaya, L. (2013). *Are productivity spillovers from Japanese FDI larger than U.S. FDI? Inter-industry evidence from Mexico*. Mexico: Universidad de Guadalajara.

Head, K., Ries, J., & Swenson, D. (1995). Agglomeration benefits and location choice: Evidence from Japanese manufacturing investments in the United States. *Journal of International Economics, 38*(4), 223–247.

Huang, H., & Wei, D. (2011). Spatial-temporal patterns and determinants of foreign direct investment in China. *Erdkunde, 65*(1), 7–23.
Hyun, J. H. (2008). A comparative analysis of transplants and industrial location of Japanese and Korean automotive industries in Europe. *International Journal of Business, 13*(3), 215–235.
INEGI. (2016). Sistema Estatal y Municipal de Bases de Datos. www.inegi.org.mx. Accessed 28 Jan 2016.
Jordaan, J. A. (2009). *Foreign direct investment, agglomeration and externalities*. Farnham: Ashgate.
Kakihara, T., & Guzman-Anaya, L. (2014). Factores de Localización de la Inversión Extranjera Directa Japonesa en México. In T. Okabe & S. Carrillo (Eds.), *Relaciones México-Japón en el contexto del Acuerdo de Asociación Económica* (pp. 135–173). Mexico: Juan Pablos Editor.
Kotabe, M. (1993). The promotional roles of the state government and Japanese manufacturing direct investment in the United States. *Journal of Business Research, 27*(2), 131–146.
Lichtensztejn, S. (2014). La Inversión Extranjera Directa en México (1980–2011) Aspectos Cuantitativos y Cualitativos. In S. Lichtensztejn (Ed.), *Inversión Extranjera en Países Emergentes en Transición* (pp. 101–197). Mexico: Universidad Veracruzana.
Little, J. S. (1978, July/August). Locational decisions of foreign direct investors in the United States. *New England Economic Review*, pp. 43–63.
Luger, M. I., & Shetty, S. (1985). Determinants of foreign plant start-ups in the United States: Lessons for policymakers in the southeast. *Vanderbilt Journal of Transnational Law, 18*(2), 223–245.
Mair, A., Florida, R., & Kenney, M. (1988). The new geography of automobile production: Japanese transplants in North America. *Economic Geography, 64*(4), 352–373.
Marshall, A. (1920). *Principles of economics* (8th ed.). London: Macmillan.
Reid, N. (1995). Just-in-time inventory control and the economic integration of Japanese-owned manufacturing plants with the country, state and national economies of the United States. *Regional Studies, 29*(4), 345–355.
Romero, Q. L., & Andres-Rosales, R. (2014). *Técnicas Modernas de Análisis Regional*. México: Plaza y Valdés.
Smith, D. F., & Florida, R. (1994). Agglomeration and industrial location: An econometric analysis of Japanese-affiliated manufacturing establishments in automotive-related industries. *Journal of Urban Economics, 36*(1), 23–41.
Toyo Keizai Inc. (2014). *Kaigai Shinshutsu Kigyou Souran*. Tokyo: Toyo Keizai Inc.
Toyo Keizai Inc. (2015). *Kaigai Shinshutsu Kigyou Souran*. Tokyo: Toyo Keizai Inc.
UNDP. (2016). *Índice de Desarrollo Municipal*. www.mx.undp.org/. Accessed 3 Feb 2016.
Wakasugi, R. (2005). The effects of Chinese eegional conditions on the location choice of Japanese affiliates. *The Japanese Economic Review, 56*(4), 390–407.
Woodward, D. P. (1992). Locational determinants of Japanese manufacturing start-ups in the United States. *Southern Economic Journal, 58*(3), 690–708.
Yamawaki, H. (1991). Exports and foreign distributional activities: Evidence on Japanese firms in the United States. *Review of Economics and Statistics, 73*(2), 294–300.
Zhou, C., Delios, A., & Yang, J. (2002). Locational determinants of Japanese foreign direct investment in China. *Asia Pacific Journal of Management, 19*(1), 63–86.

Chapter 4
Spillovers of Japanese Automotive Companies' Activities in the State of Aguascalientes

Emma Mendoza Martínez

Abstract Nissan was the first Japanese company to arrive in Mexico, in 1959. Initially established as a distributor of the Datsun brand, it soon converted into a whole car manufacturer. However, it was not until 1982, with the establishment of its first manufacturing plant in Aguascalientes and a shared investment of more than 1.3 billion dollars that Nissan became a real icon of Japanese companies in Mexico. The assignment, in 2013, of 2 billion U.S. dollars for the establishment of its second production plant—the largest foreign investment in the history of the country—was the second major step undertaken by Nissan. This impressive expansion was, in part, the result of the close interaction between Nissan and its first-level—Tier 1—suppliers, many of which were established in Mexico almost simultaneously with the company. However, a no less important factor that contributed to these achievements was the effort made by the State Government of Aguascalientes in attracting and providing a strong support to Nissan for its operations in the state. As a host of this long-term flow of investment from Nissan, the State of Aguascalientes has not only experienced an important economic growth, but also has benefited from the development of local suppliers and their integration into the Global Value Chains (GVC) and the demonstration effect exerted on local companies.

Keywords Automotive industry · Mexico · Japan · Foreign direct investment spillovers · Small and medium size enterprises

E. Mendoza Martínez (✉)
Pacific Studies Department, University of Guadalajara, Zapopan, Mexico
e-mail: emma.mendoza@gmail.com

M. Falck-Reyes, L. Guzman-Anaya (eds.), *Japanese Direct Investment in Mexico's Transport Equipment Sector*, New Frontiers in Regional Science: Asian Perspectives 22,
https://doi.org/10.1007/978-981-10-7718-0_4

4.1 Introduction[1]

The first wave of foreign investment in the Mexican automotive industry came from U.S. companies—Ford, General Motors and Chrysler—in the second half of the 1970s, just when Japanese automotive industries were threatening to flood the U.S. market. For this reason, U.S. companies felt the need to modernize their technological base and began to increase their investments in new production plants in the north of Mexico. In 1981, General Motors established an assembly plant and an engine plant in Ramos Arizpe, Coahuila, and Chrysler set an engine plant in the same place. Later, Ford built two plants: one for production of engines in Chihuahua, in 1983, and an assembly plant in Hermosillo, Sonora, in 1986. In this sense, American companies that had set up production facilities on the Northern border of Mexico during the 1980s marked in a decisive manner the behavior of the automotive sector—both in the Mexican and the international markets—betting on exportations. Afterwards, the signing of free trade agreements with the United States in 1994, and with the European Union in 2000, and a simultaneous liberalization of tariff barriers, facilitated the integration of Mexico into international markets. The transplantation of foreign companies into Mexico, the establishment of alliances or joint ventures between Mexican and foreign companies, along with the creation of Mexican firms aiming to support the operations of the incoming companies, became all a ground on which Mexican enterprises, engineers and technicians could acquire new knowledge and new production practices, which was especially evident in the automotive sector.

Moreover, the industrial development and foreign trade programs promoted by the Mexican government since the 1980s, such as the National Program for Industrial Development (1984–1988; Pronafice), the National Program of Industrial Modernization and Foreign Trade (1990–1994; Pronamice), and the Program for Industrial Policy (1996–2000; Propice), sought to provide special motivation to certain sectors by promoting regional specialization. These programs also looked to integrate small and medium-sized enterprises (SMEs) into the productive sectors of the country (Lara 2004:39–47).

As historical evidence has shown, in countries with high levels of development, SMEs have played an important role in strengthening those nations competitiveness, allowing them to participate in global value chains and to diversify their export basket. Moreover, SMEs can be sources of innovation and modernization, serving as points of convergence for business strategies and public policies that are looking to achieve common goals and compatibility with international trends.

In Mexico, the National Council for Micro, Small and Medium-sized Enterprises (MSMEs) was established in 1995 with the objective of designing and coordinating supportive measures, developing tools for specialized and integral advice, stimulating the association and interconnection of large companies, and setting strategies for the promotion of direct and indirect exportations (Lara 2004:51). During the

[1] In the following, the names of Mexican enterprises, programs and organizations are presented after their acronyms in Spanish.

current term of office (2012–2018), the Federal Government has tried to intertwine the objectives for national development with the objectives for national innovation through the Program for Innovative Development 2013–2018, by recognizing that "in a knowledge-based economy, innovation and abilities have become the countries' new capital" (Secretaría de Economía 2013:35).

In line with the country's goals, the National Council of Science and Technology (CONACyT) and the state governments formulated the state and regional Agendas of Innovation with the aim to "support federal entities and regions of the country in defining strategies of intelligent specialization for driving innovation, and scientific and technological development based on economic vocation and local capabilities" (CONACyT 2015a). Particularly, the automotive and auto parts industry we focus on in this Chapter, has been featured as an important player in the Agenda of Innovation of Aguascalientes (CONACyT 2014), due to the weight this industry has gained as an attractor of investments for the entity in recent years. This Agenda set out the most important guidelines for the state government in terms of designing economic and industrial policies during the last 6-year term (2010–2016).

Aguascalientes's case is special in that foreign direct investment into the automotive sector started since 1982 with the establishment of Nissan in the entity, so we can analyze the effect of the long-term presence of this company and its foreign subsidiaries on local suppliers, and on the Aguascalientes development, in a wider sense.

Externalities brought by FDI have been the subject of an extensive list of studies, focused on different aspects of the interaction between arriving companies and actors from the host country. These externalities are brought through (1) demonstration effects, (2) labor turnover, (3) intra- and inter-industry linkages, describing each of these channels ways in which the very presence of multinational corporations in a host country influences the activity of local enterprises (Altenburg 2000; Saggi 2002). However, country-specific studies diverge in the estimates of the outcomes of FDI, and the extent of the benefits it generate, and also on the reasons of the discrepancies observed in different countries.

Thus, a research question that guided the present study was: in which way have the externalities generated by Japanese automotive companies operations been reflected in the economy of the state of Aguascalientes as a receptor of FDI?

Particularly, we were interested in determining how did the foreign direct investment Japanese firms, through spillovers arising from their presence influenced (1) the academic sector in conditions of a strong deficit of skilled workers, (2) the establishment of research and development centers, (3) the development of local suppliers, (4) the competitiveness of enterprises outside the automotive sector, and (5) on the innovation process.

To conduct our empirical study, we relied primarily on on-site interviews to representatives of the Nissan's suppliers, both of Japanese and Mexican origin. Similarly was obtained the information to analyze the role of the presence of Nissan in Aguascalientes in the development of the academic research and educational programs, as also in the elaboration of specific programs by governments of different levels, aimed at supporting the integration of local small and medium-size enterprises to the production chain of Nissan and its major suppliers. In total we interviewed 9 representatives from government-related organisms, 5 from the academic sector, 10 from the industrial sector, and 3 representatives of private and public research institutes. The interviews were conducted between February and November 2016.

Throughout the study, we compare our empirical results with a wider analysis conducted previously by J.A. Jordaan for the Mexican manufacturing industry, and resumed in his book *Foreign Direct Investment: Agglomeration and Externalities* (2009). After an extensive review in which the effects of FDI in different states of Mexico were estimated, Jordan focused on the interaction between FDI and domestic companies in the state of Nuevo Leon, Mexico, to examine the premise that the presence of foreign companies serves as a positive factor, stimulating the development of local companies. We found that many of the observations made by Jordaan are still valid and define the interaction outcome between FDI and local companies.

This Chapter is organized as follows: the second section is an overview of the rise of the automotive industry in Aguascalientes; it also contains a brief reference to the establishment of Nissan and its first suppliers in the entity. The third section offers a characterization of the Aguascalientes state through the economic benefits generated by the automotive sector. The fourth section focuses on: (1) how has the automotive industry in Aguascalientes evolved after the creation, by the State and Federal Governments, of supporting programs aimed to develop local suppliers (2) the explanation of how have the needs of Japanese companies in the automotive sector encouraged the Mexican government to further develop the support industry in the country, and (3) the observation that a greater linkage of universities and research centers with local companies is fundamental for achieving a better productive and competitive performance by the latter, which, combined with government support, helps to create the so called triple helix. The fifth section deals with the link between FDI companies and local suppliers. Particularly, the case of the relation between Tachi-S and MICSA and MAEN is approached. Finally, in the sixth section Nissan is presented as a key factor defining the Aguascalientes's automotive specialization. Conclusions follow.

4.2 The Establishment of Nissan in Aguascalientes

Nissan was the first Japanese company to arrive in Mexico, in 1959. At the beginning Nissan started operating as a car distributor of the Datsun brand, and then, 2 years later, set up as an independent company, Nissan Mexicana S.A. de C.V. In 1966 Nissan started operations in Cuernavaca, in Morelos State, being this its first plant established overseas (Corporativo Nissan n.d.). Nissan became the first Japanese automotive firm to compete with U.S. car makers, which had a longer previous history in Mexico. As time went by, Nissan became an icon of Japanese companies in Mexico. In 1982, the company decided to establish its second plant in Mexico with a shared investment of 1.3 billion dollars by the company and its suppliers, following the attractive conditions offered by the Aguascalientes's government.

José Zapiain—Head of the Automotive Engineering Department at the Autonomous University of Aguascalientes—mentions: "In those years, when

Nissan established in Aguascalientes, it was just a transaxle and engine plant; it didn't manufacture cars yet. It was not until 1992 that the plant manufacturing the whole vehicle started operations. At that moment, economic opportunities were triggered, not only for companies linked to the automotive sector, but in general, for the local economy. Before that, the pieces and components used by the company, and everything it assembled, were brought from outside the country. For example, car painting was brought from Japan, glass sealants were imported from the United States" (J. Zapiain, UAA, interview, February 17, 2016).

4.2.1 First Nissan Suppliers

In 1992, when Nissan began assembling whole vehicles, Aguascalientes had a new government oriented towards the modernization and consolidation of industrial promotion. Two programs were supported, one for supplier development and the other for deregulation, giving Aguascalientes a competitive advantage over other entities. During the 6-year term of office of 1992 to 1998, the government managed to attract 15 Japanese companies (Lara 2004:194). Sanoh Industrial (established in 1991), INSA (in 1992), Yorozu (in 1993) and Unipress (in 1995) were among the automotive companies that arrived to Mexico. These companies had knowledge on Nissan's supply demands, so they established almost simultaneously with Nissan in Aguascalientes.

One of these companies was Industria de Asiento Superior S.A. de C.V. (INSA, later renamed as Tachi-S), also a Nissan Tier 1 supplier which assembled seats and their components. This company relocated in Aguascalientes its own—Tier 2—suppliers of Mexican and foreign origin (an example was Servicios Técnicos Profesionales MARISA S.A. de C.V., which initially operated in Mexico City, but relocated in 1994; I. Sánchez, MARISA, interview, May 6, 2016b), and later assumed the task of developing local suppliers (J. Rodríguez, Tachi-S, interview, June 9, 2016).

It is important to point out that before these new industrial poles arose in the north and central part of the country, Mexico City was the main area for economic activity, characterized by a large number of fiercely competing firms without specialization. The lack of specialization among suppliers was one of the reasons why foreign direct investment companies decreased their support to them and, on the contrary, even demanded lower costs (Jordaan 2009:134–135).

After the first stage, in which most of Nissan suppliers, Tier 1 and Tier 2 companies, arrived to Aguascalientes, the next wave of investors from Japan came in after the signing of the Japan-Mexico Economic Partnership Agreement (EPA) in 2004, which forecasted big business opportunities. However, along with envisaged opportunities, some Japanese companies also anticipated an increase in competition due to the elevated number of firms that would be located in the region. Therefore, companies such as INSA set strategies for the development of suppliers from local enterprises that would allow maintaining competitiveness through cost reduction, assurance of quality in the production and on-time delivery.

Bringing its immediate foreign suppliers to Mexico was a strategy that allowed Nissan starting operations without significant delays, which could have been critical in the fiercely competitive automotive market. Once running, however, this scheme started to maintain itself, offering limited possibilities to the incorporation of late newcomers like local MSMEs non familiar with the requirements of the automotive market. It can be stated that this situation is still preserved nowadays. Despite the existence of examples of efforts to develop local suppliers, like that of INSA, mentioned above, most Nissan's suppliers opt for importing their processes instead of developing local capabilities—a situation also common in other cutting-edge sectors like electronics and the aerospace industry (APEC Policy Support Unit 2017:20).

4.3 Economic Benefits Generated by the Establishment of the Automotive Industry in Aguascalientes

Aguascalientes is the second smallest state in Mexico, with an area of 5616 km^2 (constituting around 0.28% of the area of Mexico) and with a population of around 1,300,000 inhabitants. Nevertheless, in recent years, Aguascalientes' high indexes of industrialization, security, education and quality of life have granted it the nickname of "Mexico's little giant".

We can argue that the automotive industry has been the main driver of the Aguascalientes economic boom. However, a detailed look on the history of this small state suggests that, though the impact of the automotive industry has been indisputable, the factors that contributed to the achievement of the high scores of Aguascalientes in the economic and social indices at the Mexican nationwide level were several.

In the decade of 1940s, when the Mexican economy pursued a policy of import substitution, Aguascalientes have already had an important role in the country, contributing with 0.87% of the national GDP and having a degree of industrialization twice as high as the Mexican average (Romo Vázquez 1994). Later the economy of Aguascalientes entered a period of recession which lasted until the Mexican economy opened to foreign investment (in the 1960s and 1970s). It was starting in this last period that the economy of Aguascalientes experienced its most impressive growth, mainly in its secondary and tertiary economy sectors (which experienced, respectively, a 7- and 4-fold rise in 1990s, in comparison with the 1970s (Romo Vázquez 1994).

The strategic geographical location of Aguascalientes in the center of the country has been another key factor that contributed to the attractiveness of this state for investors. Highways and rail tracks connect it to Texas on the northern border, and to the main Mexican ports of Tampico, Veracruz, Lazaro Cardenas and Manzanillo. One of the indicators of the economic benefits that investments brought to Aguascalientes is the volume of load exchange between the state and these destinations: between 1995 and 2014 the load exchange volume by trucking increased

37%, the volume exchange by maritime transport increased 55%, while trade using railways more than doubled (Gobierno del Estado de Aguascalientes 2016). Aguascalientes also has aerial communication with national and international destinations such as Mexico City, Monterrey, Tijuana, Cancun, Puerto Vallarta, Los Angeles, Dallas and Houston.

Aguascalientes' wide network of communications has been one of the key factors that allowed this state to attain the strategic importance it has nowadays for the economy of the country, and foreign investment has been one of the pillars that supports its position at the national level. From 2010 to 2015, Aguascalientes rose from 7th to 3rd place in the national ranking of FDI *per capita* (Idem:22). The state has 19 industrial parks (11 of them—public, 6 private, and 2 municipal) (Gobierno del Estado de Aguascalientes 2014). The industrial parks are ready to receive any kind of investment and have a wide network of connections that guarantee a steady electric supply. In 2013, Nissan Motor Company made the greatest foreign investment in the history of the country, with 2 billion dollars devoted to the first stage of a new automotive complex, inaugurated in November 2013 (NissanNews.com 2014). Afterwards, in September 2015, an alliance between Renault-Nissan and Daimler laid the first cornerstone of the COMPAS plant, where Mercedes Benz and Infiniti cars will be manufactured. It had a combined investment of 1 billion dollars, which will generate 3600 direct jobs and 12,000 indirect jobs with the goal of manufacturing 230,000 Premium brand cars each year, starting from 2017 (El Universal 2015).

Besides the externalities generated by the foreign direct investment, other kind of benefits derived from such investments can be observed. An example is the increased support given by the state government to some universities in the entity. The Autonomous University of Aguascalientes, in particular, has benefited from a total of more than 581 million pesos—since 2011— allocated mainly for school activities and programs, and for the expansion of university facilities (La Jornada Aguascalientes 2016). In this sense, the Southern Campus of the university was built for hosting engineering careers oriented towards manufacturing that started in 2012.

Likewise, the government has provided financial backup for micro, small and medium-size enterprises (MSMEs) in Aguascalientes, with an investment of 1.3 billion pesos (El Heraldo Aguascalientes 2016a), with combined resources from the state government and the National Institute of the Entrepreneur (INADEM), for a total of 111 projects that benefited 32,600 companies and entrepreneurs, creating and maintaining 18,500 jobs. The conclusion of the construction of the new general hospital "Miguel Hidalgo" is one of the biggest infrastructure projects, which began to offer services at the end of 2017. The cost of building has been estimated in 1.7 million pesos, and is equipped with 200 beds (Hermosillo 2017). As for hotel infrastructure, Aguascalientes holds more than 6000 rooms, showing this parameter a sustained growth since 2011 (Gobierno del Estado de Aguascalientes 2016:141).

Some of these FDI externalities will be analyzed below in more detail.

The benefits that the entity has received—linked directly or indirectly to the growth of the automotive sector—can also be observed in different areas, such as the creation of 80,000 jobs during the 2010–2016 administration (El Heraldo Aguascalientes 2016b). This allows the state to be ranked third in terms of employment growth, above the national average (NTR Zacatecas 2016). In 2016, the Aguascalientes's GDP was nearly three times the national one, and a similar relationship is forecasted for 2017, despite the decrease in absolute terms as a result of the protectionist politics of the newly elected president Trump (Indicadores Regionales de Actividad Económica 2017). Furthermore, the entity holds the 3rd place in competitiveness at the national level, according to the data provided by the Mexican Institute of Competitiveness (La Jornada Aguascalientes 2015a).

4.4 Current Development of the Automotive Industry in Aguascalientes and the Role Different Actors Play in the Process

One of the anticipated outcomes of large FDI flows to a specialized industrial sector is the technology transfer from foreign companies to companies of the host economy. It is commonly assumed that such transfer will contribute to drive the industrial development of a hosting entity, region, or country. In the case of the automotive industry, the expectations are higher, since it is an economic sector capable of generating huge economic benefits. Certainly, the economic indicators highlight the outstanding boom that the Mexican automotive industry has experienced in recent years, and especially, the productivity observed in the Bajio region due to Nissan's establishment of its second plant, as well as of other Japanese autopart manufacturers and supplier companies. However, this rise is not reflected in an equal increase or improvement of opportunities for local Mexican companies to join the GVC. A consequence of this is that, at the national level, 90% of the parts and components required by the automotive sector are still imported (Mexico Industry 2016).

4.4.1 Programs Established by the Mexican Government

The role of the Federal Government and State Governments is crucial for the formulation of appropriate industrial policies aimed at the attraction of foreign investors and for directing investments to sectors that require to be boosted. In Mexico, the necessity of strengthening the support industry in the automotive sector was stressed since the flow of Japanese investments increased as a result of the signing of the EPA. In particular, the Japanese government, through its representatives, has expressed on several occasions the importance of strengthening this industry in Mexico, arguing that, otherwise, competitiveness would be limited. In 2007, Ambassador of Japan in Mexico Masaaki Ono warned: "the country is missing its place within the supporting industry and thus global supplying industries are looking to other nations. In order to improve the competitive advantages of Japanese firms in Mexico it is crucial to promote supplying industries in Mexican territory, as currently they are scarce and barely supply materials for Japanese assembly companies. Nowadays, Mexico is not a place for producing components as it lacks support industries, hence Japanese industries turn to other countries to do it" (CRÓNICA.com.mx 2007). In 2011, Takahiro Okazaki, General Director of JETRO, made a statement regarding this issue: "By observing the actual situation of the automotive support industry in Mexico, there are companies that do not fulfill the required standards and are not on the same level as manufacturing companies with foreign capital. Although there are excellent Mexican companies, weak points still persist, such as lack of resources, obsolete machinery and quality controls not strict enough. Therefore, some of the areas in which Mexico should drive its technological level are: cold forging, thermal processes, mold and die manufacturing, and fabrication of screws, springs, among others ..." (Okazaki 2011).

Statements of this kind and the commitments established between Mexico and Japan on cooperation matters, through the EPA, have prompted the Mexican Federal Government and local governments to extend and diversify their share portfolio, with greater financial support, administrative guidance, training and linkages to achieve the integration of a large number of SMEs within the productive chain of the automotive sector. The requirements of the industry, but also the increased international protectionism of the markets, have additionally played an important role in the formulation by the Mexican government of policies aimed at increasing the productivity of mature sectors, and at supporting the development of highly-competitive MSMEs (see in APEC Policy Support Unit 2017:4).

In the above-mentioned Aguascalientes's Agenda of Innovation for the automotive and auto parts sector, two major objectives were set: (1) to support the development of local industry in the niches of opportunity demanded by Original Equipment Manufacturers (OEMs) and Tier 1 companies; and (2) to foster the technological and innovation capacities of the sector in all the chains, focusing the efforts in the following three niches of specialization and lines of action: (a) identification and generation of technological and managerial capacities during the development of suppliers; (b) linking of human resources that work in design, R&D and engineering; and (c) creation of policies for the attraction of transnational companies' R&D centers (CONACyT 2014:18). If these goals were achieved it would confirm Jordaan's statement that "in contrast to the negative effect of regional diversity, regional specialization fosters the occurrence of positive spatial intra-industry FDI externalities" and "regions with specialized manufacturing activities possess a high level of absorbing capacity, facilitating the incorporation of positive productivity effects from FDI firms located in nearby regions" (2009:143). This last link will also be in agreement with the observations, made previously by Kokko for the Mexican manufacturing industry (1994).

Some of the programs implemented by the Federal Government and the Aguascalientes State Government during the administration (2010–2016), aimed at achieving some of the objectives mentioned above, are shown in the following table (Table 4.1).

Table 4.1 Support programs to SMEs of Aguascalientes, suppliers of the automotive sector[a]

Name of the program	Content
SEDEC/Fund to boost the automotive SMEs (Fondo Impulso PYME Automotriz) (Local program)	The project, implemented in 2015–2016, used the revenue obtained from the payroll tax (51.8 million pesos) accumulated between 2010 and 2014. By means of this fund, 58 enterprises got subsidies. Supported areas were: certification, specialized training and investment in machinery. The maximum of the subsidy was 1 million pesos or 50% of the total investment. As a condition, beneficiaries were required to create one to five new jobs, according to the grant received.
SEDEC/Aguascalientes "The Small Giant Mexican Exporter" (Local program)	This was a "networking" type event. The state government invited driving-force companies to do business with local suppliers. The Ministry of Economic Development compiled the specific requirements of the client companies, distributed them among potential suppliers and scheduled meetings. The event was supported by the program Supplier Hunter (SUHU), a database owned by ProMéxico[b], by means of which client companies upload their requirements or search directly for suppliers.
INADEM/Direct assignment programs (Federal-local program; 2016)	The Programs for Strategic Sectors and Regional Development of the National Institute of the Entrepreneur (INADEM) allow local governments to apply for a direct financial assignment addressed to a project considered as strategic for the entity. In this way, the program "Strengthening the Automotive Industry" furnished with *Enterprises Resource Planning Systems* (ERP) to 15 enterprises related to the automotive sector (INADEM n.d.).
SEDEC-ENDEAVOR/ Sinergia (Local program)	The government of Aguascalientes and the enterprise Endeavor Co. support companies that are looking for institutionalization and corporate governance. The aim is to reduce costs, achieve a better management of their resources, an adequate organization chart and get financial statements in order.
Conacyt/Mixed Funds (Fomix) (Federal-Local program)	This fund is oriented at local organizations (academic or productive) with the aim of generating economic, social and productive benefits for an entity. The "Model for the generation and consolidation of strategic human capital that meets the needs of the automotive industry of the Aguascalientes state" by the Monterrey Institute of Technology and Higher Education (ITESM) was selected in 2012. This project allowed the training of 50 engineering students in line with the requirements and needs of the automotive industry.
Conacyt/PEI (Federal program)	The Innovation Stimulus Program (PEI) seeks to promote development and technological innovation through the establishment of links between companies, universities, and research institutes as a means. In 2016, the fine blanking project by the metalworking company Metalistik and the Center of Advanced Technology (CIATEQ) was selected.
Aguascalientes Government/Progress Fund (Local program)	Local government grants loans with low interest rates of 6% *per annum*.
Factoring Programs (Federal program)	Through the Mexican Foreign Trade Bank (Bancomext), the government promotes financial support to the automotive industry, which has factoring programs with very low interest rates.

(continued)

Table 4.1 (continued)

Name of the program	Content
Nafinsa/Productive Chains (Federal program)	The National Financial Institution for Development (Nacional Financiera S.N.C./Nafinsa) has a factoring program named "Productive Chains" that supports potential suppliers in their linking with client companies.
Continuous improvement courses/ CECOI (local program)	The Aguascalientes Center for Competitiveness and Innovation (CECOI) offers training to local SMEs in continuous improvement systems, such as *Kaizen*[c], *Gemba*[d], *5S*[e] or *8D*[f]. CECOI also supports companies in establishing links with universities and research institutes to improve competitiveness and innovation. (L. Cedillo Díaz, CECOI, interview, March 16, 2016).

Source: Author's elaboration based mainly on the information provided by the Director of Supplier Development and Foreign Trade, Ministry of Economic Development, Aguascalientes Government, 16 February 2016.

[a]The information related to the support programs for the automotive industry in Aguascalientes was obtained from an interview with José Alfredo Díaz, Director of the Office of Supplier Development and Foreign Trade of the Secretary of Economic Development (SEDEC), Aguascalientes (February 16, 2016).

[b]A Mexican Federal Government trusteeship, that promotes trade and investment.

[c]"Change for the better".

[d]A Japanese word that literally means "the real place, used in business process improvement contexts". *Gemba* also is the factory floor in manufacturing.

[e]Sort, set in order, shine, standardize and sustain.

[f]The eight disciplines model is a problem solving approach typically employed by quality engineers or other professionals and commonly used in the automotive industry. Its purpose is to identify, correct, and eliminate recurring problems, and is useful in product and process improvement.

Unfortunately, many of these programs lack a feedback mechanism to evaluate their effectiveness. In this task the Mexican government at its different levels is aided by the academy. In 2016, the Mathematical Research Centre (CIMAT) campus in Aguascalientes carried out the survey *Factors that intervene in the competitiveness of micro, small and medium industries in Aguascalientes: "A competitive model"*. The survey comprised a sample of 86 local companies supplying parts to the automotive industry, and which have succeeded in the integration into the automotive production chain. The purpose of the study was to identify the best practices and the key factors that allowed these companies to become competitive and to be incorporated as providers in the supply chain of one of the manufacturing sectors with the highest requirements in terms of production volumes, demand for quality and delivery times (CIMAT & IDEPMEX & CASCI Instituto de Desarrollo de Proveedores de México 2016:1).

The results obtained were relevant not only for the surveyed companies, as they could identify other areas of opportunity, but also for those companies seeking to improve their performance in an increasingly competitive context, as the model offered an instrument for self-evaluation. In the analysis eight variables were taken into account: (1) production management, (2) commercial management, (3) administrative management, (4) organizational development, (5) innovation and technological vanguard, (6) environment, (7) structural aspects of the chain of value of the Original Equipment Manufacturer (OEM), and (8) government support. The result of the analysis showed that the overall index of the competitiveness of MSMEs in Aguascalientes was 7.3 points on average (out of a maximum of 10 points). The variables that achieved the highest scores were: administrative management (7.8) and environment (7.5), and those with the lowest, were: government support (6.5), and innovation and technological vanguard (6.8). The other variables fluctuated between 7.3 and 7.2 points (Idem:10–11). It was concluded, that although MSMEs have been able to participate in the automotive supply chain, they must improve their leadership skills to gain projects and increase their abilities to attract and develop qualified human resources. In this sense, "if a company knows what determines its capacity to absorb the externalities of FDI, the company managers can make better decisions considering the improvement of efficiency and performance. On the other hand, people who make decisions in government can also identify which industries are most likely to benefit from the effects of FDİ and make adjustments to their tax incentives" (Sánchez-Sellero et al. 2014:430).

The availability of a significant number of public programs reflect an increased interest of the Mexican government in developing a strong supporting infrastructure of highly-skilled MSMEs. Albeit, it is arguable the extent to which these steps correspond to preventive measures undertaken by the government itself, and not just to a reaction to the pressing requests of the foreign companies investing in the automotive sector. Particularly, while in several of the public programs mentioned above foreign enterprises played an important guiding role, there is much room for improvement of the coordination of the efforts amongst the different branches of the government, to which the access of these companies is much less limited. An example of this is the Mexican regulatory and taxing systems, characterized by their complexity in comparison with those in more business-friendly countries (see in APEC Policy Support Unit 2017:26).

It has also been observed that some of these programs need optimization, like increased funding, improvement of the efficiency of their management and the establishment of propper evaluation and feedback mechanisms. Moreover, most these programs are weakly coordinated, which translate into redundance of governmental efforts, inefficients spending of scarce public resources, and confusion amongst MSMEs (APEC Policy Support Unit 2017:27).

4.4.2 The Role of the Japanese Government in the Establishment of Mexican Suppliers

The EPA between Japan and Mexico includes a special chapter dedicated to bilateral cooperation that stresses the strengthening of the support industry in Mexico. Accordingly, the Japanese Government, through the Japan International Cooperation Agency (JICA), has offered various support programs for the automotive sector in Mexico (SE/ProMéxico 2015:52).

During the period 2012–2015, JICA carried out the program for *Strengthening of the Supply Chain*[2] in the states of Guanajuato, Queretaro and Nuevo Leon. In this occasion, Aguascalientes was not included in this program as it was considered that the network of suppliers around Nissan was well developed in the entity, and JICA's objective was to expand the positive effects generated by regional specialization. The program was applied not only in Guanajuato where Honda, Mazda and Toyota investments were secured, but also in Queretaro and Nuevo Leon, glimpsing the possibility that some suppliers could establish in some of these states (A. Ríos, JICA Mexico, interview, June 7, 2016). However, SMEs located in Aguascalientes, despite not being included in the JICA program, have received contracts and other kind of benefits from the newly established companies such as Toyota, Mazda, Kasai, among others.

Another initiative supported by JICA is the *Senior Volunteers* program in which senior experts visited enterprises to share their knowledge and experience with local companies, in order to improve their processes and efficiency. Unfortunately, in the opinion of some entrepreneurs the results were not as satisfactory as expected because it was not possible to apply the program in depth due to time constraints, since the volunteers were permanently residing in other states, where the program was carried out (H. Sánchez, Metalistik, interview, May 5, 2016a; A. Gómez, Industrias DMU, interview, May 6, 2016). JICA, however, had previously granted Aguascalientes with support programs that allowed government officials and local entrepreneurs the opportunity to take training courses in Japan, with the aim of forming an automotive cluster in Aguascalientes (J.A. Díaz, SEDEC, interview, February 16, 2016).

A program that is currently being implemented is the Human Resources Formation Project (*Monozukuri*) for the Automotive Industry in the Bajio Region. This program is part of the project "Automotive Manufacturing" that started in 2016 as a collaboration between The National College of Professional Technical Education (Conalep, Mexico) and JICA, and will be implemented in the states of Aguascalientes, Guanajuato and Querétaro, in the school sites of Aguascalientes, Celaya, Irapuato and San Juan del Río (El Heraldo Aguascalientes 2016c).

At present, two groups of 35 students are participating in Aguascalientes in the first generation of this program. Although the program, that lasts 3 years, took off in August 2016, the JICA staff began to train teachers 1 year before, and they will stay in Aguascalientes until the first generation of students graduate in June, 2019 (El Heraldo Aguascalientes 2016d).

At present, two groups of 35 students are the participants of the first generation in the Aguascalientes campus. The 3-year program took off in August 2016, however the JICA personnel began training teachers 1 year before, and they will remain in Aguascalientes until June 2019, when the first generation of students graduate (El Heraldo Aguascalientes 2016d). This new career will focus on the following objectives: (1) training of highly competitive students, (2) training of teachers; (3) close link with the automotive industry; and (4) school workshops in accordance with the automotive technology.

[2]Leo Guzman-Anaya approached this topic in depth in Chap. 3. Locational Determinants of Japanese Automotive FDI in Mexico: A Spatial Analysis.

Besides JICA, the Japan External Trade Organization (JETRO), in collaboration with ProMéxico, the Offices of Economic Development from different states and the automotive clusters in different states are working to promote better links among companies from both countries. Since 2010, JETRO has maintained a database of Mexican companies that could serve as potential suppliers for the Japanese companies established in Mexico, the United States and Japan. Even though the catalogue can only be consulted by Japanese firms, the Mexican companies included in it can also improve their business opportunities. JETRO experts working in the automotive sector are generally those who identify potential Mexican companies that could eventually become suppliers of Japanese companies. On its website JETRO also extends the invitation to Mexican companies to approach the organization (JETRO Mexico 2016).

4.4.3 The Role of Universities and Research Centers

4.4.3.1 Universities

As mentioned in the Introduction, innovation is considered to be one of the most important drivers of the modern economy. To foster innovation, governments and other institutions seek the establishment of an alliance between the industry and academic research, and look for the complementarity of their goals. To achieve this purpose, it is important to guarantee not only a certain number of universities involved in engineering programs but also an improved communication and collaboration among engineers, technicians, researchers and students of higher education institutions.

In Aguascalientes, the first efforts to bring to life technical and engineering programs were done by the Aguascalientes Regional Institute of Technology, later renamed as the Aguascalientes Institute of Technology (ITA), established in 1967, and the Autonomous University of Aguascalientes (UAA), opened in 1973 (UAA 2016). From these first steps, the current higher education and technical structure began to be constituted, comprising–at present–a total of 32 universities in the state.

The real boom for technological and engineering programs linked with the automotive industry started when the Nissan A2 plant was built. It became clear that an increased number of specialists would be required. Thus, the government together with Nissan agreed on the importance of building a new campus for the UAA focused on Automotive Engineering, Mechanical Design, Robotics, Industrial Manufacturing and Automation. This new generation of programs took off in 2012.

The Polytechnic University of Aguascalientes (UPA), established in 2002, is another institution that follows this new education policy. Nowadays, it offers majors in Electronic Engineering, Industrial Engineering, Mechanical Engineering, Mechatronic Engineering, and a degree in International Business Management.

The above mentioned universities are continuously reviewing and updating their programs with the objective to keep in line with the needs and demands of the companies in Aguascalientes, but also in accordance with the international tendencies. Students also are involved in learning a second and a third language and in acquiring and improving different skills in order to be prepared for continuous technological changes and increasing competitive conditions.

To the above public institutions it must be added the private university, the Monterrey Institute of Technology and Higher Education (ITESM) that since its beginnings has been oriented at teaching technological and administrative programs. From 2010, the Aguascalientes Campus of ITESM has housed the Centre for Development of the Automotive Industry in Mexico (CeDIAM), whose Directive Board is constituted by representatives of Nissan and five other companies—Sensata, Donaldson, Calsonic, Jatco and Flextronics. The purpose of this Center is to integrate the needs of the automotive industry into the ITESM's educational programs. To this aim, the members of the Directive Board express in advance their needs and the directions of the expected future development of their companies (L. Pérez Abreu, CeDIAM, interview, March 8, 2016 and Christopher Falcón 2016). Among other functions, CeDIAM also provides training to related companies in areas such as solidwork design, packing and tool designs.

A spillover effect derived from the synergy between industrial agglomerations of the automotive sector and the universities, is that a large number of graduate students from different disciplines have the chance to be employed in their own town by a foreign company, receiving benefits such as knowledge and training. For Aguascalientes, this practice is already in course, however, in order to guarantee a successful alliance it is important to keep up a continuous effort in strengthening the university programs, in increasing the number of graduate students, and in enhancing collaborations with local enterprises.

At present, companies compete for newly graduated engineers, as their supply is not enough to cover the foreign enterprise demand. Companies like Nissan and Jatco have already started programs with local universities to carry out collaborative programs, in order to integrate students in the last stage of their bachelor studies. Students are usually incorporated in projects of optimization and improvement of the company's processes (La Jornada Aguascalientes 2015b). These programs benefit students but also companies because the latter have the opportunity to train students according to their own needs. Otherwise, the company has to start this process after hiring them, increasing training expenditures.

Consequently, the increasing of the universities' capacity, the consolidation of study programs, the strengthening of research centers and specialization of human resources have been priority policies for the Aguascalientes State Government, since they contribute to consolidate the industrial specialization of the state.

4.4.3.2 The Role of Research Centers

Along with the alliance between knowledge-producing universities and industry, the proliferation of research centers is another feature of the recent tendencies to foster innovation. The positive externalities derived from FDI companies will be higher when the recipient country has a technological base, including not only the previous *know-how* local companies had, but also universities and research centers as a critical component of the country's technological infrastructure. Even more, if adequate industrial policies and support programs are provided by the government, all these elements could contribute to a proper functioning of the so called "Triple Helix" (Cabrero and Orihuela 2012).

The state of Aguascalientes houses important research centers under the auspice of CONACyT. And although they are not strictly specialized in the automotive industry, some of their activities are specifically focused on this sector. As already mentioned, the Center for Advanced Technology (CIATEQ), Mathematical Research Centre (CIMAT) and the Centre for Optic Research (CIO) are the core of this nucleus of research centers in Aguascalientes. Under the federal and state policy to foster innovation, in 2016 one of the priorities was the "Strengthening of high specialization laboratories for the automotive sector". Then, substantial resources derived from the Mixed Fund of CONACyT and the state of Aguascalientes have been allocated to (1) the creation at CIMAT of a highly specialized laboratory in statistical engineering focused on the development and innovation of the automotive industry, (2) to strengthening at CIATEQ of laboratories for mechanical construction, information technologies and measurement for the design and manufacture of tooling for the automotive sector, and (3) to the implementation at CIO of a laboratory for optical trials in the automotive and auto-parts industry (CONACyT 2015b).

On its hand, CeDIAM established in 2010 a laboratory to carry out packing and crating tests that are the core activities of the Centre. The laboratory caters not only Nissan's orders for packing and transportation trials but also Volkswagen's and General Motors' ones. "When the vehicles of these companies do not pass or do not satisfactorily fulfill the simulations trials, CeDIAM provides assistance and guidance in packing and design for packing. Likewise, as one of Nissan objectives is to reduce, on an annual base, the costs of the pieces used for assembling, CeDIAM proposes projects to improve efficiency. In this way, it contributes to achieve the company goals" (L. Pérez Abreu, CeDIAM, interview, March 8, 2016 and Christopher Falcon 2016).

Besides packing and crating programs, CeDIAM offers courses on Nissan's technical norms. As automotive companies require their suppliers to follow specific requirements, it is important to offer them training and update courses. One example is the Alliance New Product Quality Procedure (ANPQP) methodology which is used by Nissan for securing quality for purchased parts across its supply chain. Programs are mainly oriented to Nissan Tier 1 and Tier 2 suppliers all over the country—most of them foreign companies, but Mexican local companies and even small workshops are sometimes included. In this way, CeDIAM participates in programs for the development of suppliers in areas such as 3D design with SolidWorks and tooling design, fabrication and maintenance. Hitherto, Nissan has been facing problems to find large Mexican tooling companies, as only two or three such suppliers can be found in the country. So, it has to import tooling from Japan, even though the production costs increase significantly. Hence, the company is looking to expand its programs to develop these type of suppliers in Mexico.

The existence of centers like the above mentioned, that carry out research, development and innovation (R&D+I), is essential for the technological development of the region and the country. However, according to CONACyT, for the Mexican economy it would be also desirable that transnational companies establish this kind of centers with the participation of Mexican researchers. If it happens, intelligent FDI will trigger innovation capabilities in Aguascalientes and generate a higher added value for the companies in the sector (CONACyT 2014:23).

In this sense, in 2016, CONACyT along with the Aguascalientes Government and a consortium of public research centers belonging to CONACyT, began to develop the Aguascalientes Center for Innovation and Technology Transfer for the Automotive Sector (CITTAA, in Spanish). The project, led first by CIO, will identify the main areas of opportunity for the local automotive industry in order to promote the incorporation of local companies in the automotive supply chain (González 2016). Therefore, CITTAA would be oriented to an institutional way of technology transfer.

For the international technology transfer process to take place, appropriate national policies and a corresponding legal framework are required. Furthermore, technology transfer has played a significant role in international trade and increased the involvement of different countries in the flow of goods and services across national boundaries. For the case of manufacturing industries, technology knowledge is classified as capital-embodied and labor-embodied. In the automotive industry capital-embodied technology relates to production processes like casting, forging, metal-cutting, welding, pressing, etc. Labor-embodied technology, on its hand, includes: (1) skills and know-hows of specific processes, (2) the ability to understand capital-embodied technology, (3) the capacity to design or re-design products, processes and plants, and (4) the ability to innovate and to develop new production techniques (Irawati 2012:125).

In Aguascalientes, the Mexican company DMU Industries is a representative case of labor-embodied technology transfer. The CEO of the company worked during some time for Tachi-S (see below), later he quitted the company and went to the United States to work in other companies. After having increased his knowledge, skills and experience, he returned to Mexico and started his own business specialized on plastic injection. As he had kept the relationship with Tachi-S, he received support from the company for the establishment of his own enterprise focused on the manufacturing of plastic parts for the automotive industry. At present, DMU Industries is one of Tachi-S main suppliers in Aguascalientes (A. Gómez, Industrias DMU, interview, May 6, 2016). More widely, inter-firm labor turnover in Mexico has been pointed as one of the mechanisms of technology transfer and creation of SMEs in several manufacturing sectors, through observation of the operations of foreign-owned firms (Jordaan 2009:3). Nonetheless, it is desirable that domestic companies after having received a technology transfer input be able to develop their own technological or innovative projects.

As a concluding remark to this section we should mention that, despite the efforts of the universities and research centers in creating a suitable environment for the development of local suppliers for the automotive industry, a general problem, complicating the achievement of this goal, is an average low level of education amongst employees of Mexican MSMEs, including those not involved in the automotive industry. It is cited that of the 11.5 million people employed in Mexican MSMEs only 30% have completed a preparatory school for higher education, only 15% counting with a higher education background. In addition, of the total of MSMEs, which in the automotive sector are expected to play the key role in the self-incorporation into the production chains of the multinational enterprises, only 13% provide training to employees (APEC Policy Support Unit 2017:24). This characteristic of Mexican MSMEs comes together with additional cultural barriers to their growth, namely, the preference for supplying less sophisticated industries instead of those ones that require long-term planning together with patience and commitment (APEC Policy Support Unit 2017:24). Thus, another required step for the successful development of local suppliers will be the gradual outgrowth of "traditional" MSMEs by more ambitious ones, with a growth-oriented vision.

4.5 Link Between FDI Companies and Local Suppliers. The Case of Tachi-S with MICSA (Later MAEN)

Although Tachi-S is not the only company that has developed suppliers in Aguascalientes, this company is highly acknowledged for having propitiated an adequate productive integration with local companies. Incorporation of local SMEs by Tachi-S not only exemplifies the demonstration effect by a Japanese firm on local companies, but it is also a clear example of the ripple effect from the benefited Mexican enterprises on other local companies.

INSA, as Tachi-S was originally named, was founded in Aguascalientes in 1991 as a joint venture of Tachi-S Co. Ltd. and Nissan Mexicana with the initial purpose of producing and supplying seats for cars assembled in the Nissan Aguascalientes plant, starting from 1992 (INSA 2016). Since the beginning INSA made efforts in relocating its suppliers and in replacing imported car components. However, the strategy to develop local suppliers took off during 2004–2005 years. INSA approached local companies that already had experience in the automotive sector but had to improve their production and management processes through specialized training.

In those days, the Mexican local company Manufacturas Industriales, S.A. de C.V. (MICSA) was established by three former employees of an U.S. company that was close to bankruptcy. These engineers, with experience in the field and with entrepreneurial spirit, invited 16 other workers and constituted the company. At that time, without any subsidy or some support by the government, they started the business buying used machinery with their own resources. The company was one of the enterprises selected by INSA to be developed as a supplier. The CEO of MICSA explains that: "developing suppliers is not as easy as some firms point out. Some companies that say they develop suppliers, but what they do is to choose the most skilled, with better capabilities and experience. However, INSA employees went to our facilities; they helped us to implement quality systems, systems for production assurance, product planning and engineering. They taught us how to fill the formats and how to use them, how to develop a production process and how to control it. Depending on the area, in some cases, it took weeks, and in others, like production, it took months. And, when they considered we were ready, they left us to work by ourselves" (C. Pérez Cerros, MaindSteel & Grupo MAEN, interview, March 8, 2016).

"2005 Tachi-S's strategy of relocating parts and developing suppliers was a bet that worked. And it worked very well, because they could have a better supplier platform, better control over the materials they obtained from different companies, and, therefore, they reduced costs. From this Tachi-S's project, 6 or 8 local companies were created" (Ibidem), MICSA among them.

In 2013, MICSA, renamed as MaindSteel, together with other companies supported by Tachi-S, created the industrial group Grupo MAEN (Manufacturing Automotive Enterprises Network), that later on continued increasing the number of its members.

Following Tachi-S's example to relocate parts-producing companies and to develop local suppliers that contributed to the good position of the company as a Tier 1 supplier, MICSA has also shared its knowledge and expertise with other similar local companies. Although MICSA was born and developed within the automotive industry, with time it has spread its production to different sectors. What was the key factor that allowed it to develop these initiatives? The answer to this important question is the application of the high quality standards demanded by the automotive sector to other production sectors.

Nowadays, around 50% of the MICSA's production goes to the automotive sector, and the rest is absorbed by other markets such as display cases, chain stores, casinos, telecommunications, beverages, food. MICSA has supplied its products to big firms and projects began to surpass its own capacities. Hence, MICSA asked for support other local companies involved in the automotive sector, because of their familiarity with quality systems. These companies know how to manufacture car components, how to control and how to deliver good quality, no matter the sector or the client. That situation contributed to building confidence, not only because of the quality systems implemented, but also because everything we requested would be worked, manufactured, and developed under the automotive framework" (Ibidem).

The quality system in the automotive sector is a topic that must be highlighted because in other industrial sectors it is not that strict. Moreover, companies that follow the standards of the automotive sector are likely to penetrate other sectors like aeronautics or medical industry that also require high quality standards. Thus, demonstration effects derived from FDI companies might have a positive spillover effects even higher than expected. "After the collaborative model established by MICSA, a number of companies have been integrated and Grupo MAEN was formally established in 2013. Member companies shared engineering, experience, capacities, raw materials, equipment and everything they could, and it worked well. As a result, now, more than thirty companies constitute the group" (Ibidem) and it continues growing in investment, technical and human capacity. Grupo MAEN offers products and services in areas such as sheetmetal, laser cutting, printing, tube bending, bent wire, fiberglass, plastic extrusion, plastic injection, welded assembly, electrostatic painting, electrolytic galvanizing, automation and mechanization, among others (Grupo MAEN 2016).

The relationship between Tachi-S and MaindSteel is a clear example of the positive externalities originated from FDI. However, this is not an average case of the relations established between multinational and domestic companies, but just one of the few cases of successful technology transfer. The positive result was propitiated by meeting two specific requirements, mentioned previously by several researchers in the field. First, MICSA engineers and technicians had a previous knowledge base for the operation in the sector. They just needed to specialize in some areas, and obtain experience, but possessed an adequate capacity of absorption of the knowledge they received. Second, a technological gap between both companies existed, so there was no direct competition between them. MICSA was less technologically developed than INSA. Furthermore, Tachi-S—the global corporate of INSA—already counted with previous experience in other countries where it established subsidiary companies. Related to this case, Jordaan states regarding the Mexican manufacturing industry: "the interaction variable between inter-regional intra-industry FDI externalities and technological differences between FDI and Mexican firms is positively associated with labor productivity of Mexican firms. This finding indicates that large technological differences between FDI and Mexican firms foster the materialization of positive FDI effects" (Jordaan 2009:143).

At present, Mexican companies contribute with 85% of the supply needs of Tachi-S, making a great difference with the 40% it amounted 10 years ago (J. Rodríguez, Tachi-S, interview, June 9, 2016). We should note, however, that these numbers do not refer to companies of Mexican origin, but companies located in Mexico with national registration. The strategies followed by enterprises like Tachi-S generate mutual trade benefits, both for FDI enterprises and for local companies. Benefits for MICSA have been widely stated, but INSA has also increased the number of its plants in Mexico. "It used to have only two manufacturing plants (one that made seats for Honda, in Guadalajara and other working for Nissan in Guadalajara), and one service plant (the textile headliner plant in Zacatecas). Today, however, Tachi-S holds eight manufacturing plants in Mexico, one center of engineering development, and two joint ventures—one with FTMEX and other with CITEX. It is also important to note that all of Tachi-S facilities are operated, administered, and headed by Mexican people" (C. Pérez Cerros, MaindSteel & Grupo MAEN, interview, March 8, 2016). Undoubtedly, this is a good example of an efficient productive integration.

4.6 Nissan's Presence in Aguascalientes as a Factor of Specialization for the Bajio Region

Agglomeration has been recognized in the literature as a factor contributing to the attraction of foreign investment companies to the host country (Barry et al. 2003). The presence of Nissan in Aguascalientes has undoubtedly been a decisive factor in defining this state's specialization. The story begun when in 1982 Nissan was established as an engine and transaxle company. Ten years later, it was reinforced as a company that assembled the whole vehicle. And two decades later, the firm invested 2 billion dollars for the construction of the A2 plant, triggering an increasing flow of investment to Aguascalientes and its neighboring states, both by foreign and Mexican capital.

The consolidation of Nissan in Mexico, the sales volumes in Mexico and abroad, and the new large investments were fundamental factors for creating an environment of trust that prompted investments by other companies: Honda in Celaya, and Mazda in Salamanca, in the Guanajuato state (2014); Renault-Nissan Daimler in Aguascalientes (2017); and Toyota, in Apaseo El Grande, Guanajuato, planned to start in 2019. The boom of investment spurred the expansion and proliferation of industrial agglomerations and vice versa—the industrial parks and industry agglomerations attracted new investments, so we can consider each of these results as part of the FDI externalities.

Another topic, not directly related to the demonstration effect on other firms, but linked to the FDI externalities, is the expansion and improvement of infrastructure works in the entities and the country. Highways, train rails, ports, among others, as well as interconnection of service networks are examples of the infrastructure the Mexican government has sought to offer, to improve the degree of integration and the commercial logistic competitiveness. A good illustration is the Industrial Logistic Corridors such as the CLIAB (Logistic Corridor of the Bajio Automotive Industry) that includes the Southern Industrial Zone of Aguascalientes; the Inner Port Silao, in Guanajuato; the Industrial Complexes of Silao, Celaya and Salamanca, also located in Guanajuato; and the Industrial Park Querétaro, in Queretaro state (Moreno-Codina 2015: 13–34).

4.7 Conclusions

It should be recognized that in the Aguascalientes's dilemma of giving more support to SMEs, or investing instead in infrastructure and services to become attractive for foreign investment, it is easier to focus on the second option than on giving a boost to local SMEs, which were workshops or small family companies that needed a longer and more complicated process of training that would allow them to fulfill the standards of competitiveness that multinational companies required. Today, despite some advances in leveling this situation, many of such requirements still cannot be successfully fulfilled because Mexican SMEs are not able to allocate large amounts of resources to high risk investments. Another important challenge for local SMEs, is that becoming a supplier of the automotive industry implies the need for a continuous reduction of production costs.

An obvious disadvantage in the case of Aguascalientes is the absence of an automotive cluster, similar to those existing in the states of Guanajuato, Queretaro or Nuevo Leon. The existence of a cluster facilitates the dialogue between the different sectors involved, by exposing the needs, plans and prospective of each of the members constituting it. For the local companies in Aguascalientes it would be of great importance to be integrated in such a cluster, in order to have the support of an industrial group that could act as their representative. To some extent, this objective has been achieved by companies that are part of Grupo MAEN, or part of the Grupo de Industrias del Ramo Automotriz de Aguascalientes (GIRAA). Nevertheless, currently there is no organization that could represent, as a whole, the automotive industry of Aguascalientes.

One of the possible reasons for the delay in the formation of a cluster in Aguascalientes is the absence of a competitor for Nissan, allowing the latter to impose its own model of production and conditions on its suppliers. In Jordaan's classification of FDI companies according to their age and interaction with local suppliers, Nissan could be classified as a first generation company, both for its long-time presence in Aguascalientes, and for the relation with its suppliers, oriented towards satisfying its own needs. Meanwhile, Mazda and Honda could be considered second generation companies, because they were established recently, and because linkage strategies with their suppliers have been more diverse. First generation transnational companies are characterized by yielding less positive spillovers to the host economy in comparison with new generation companies. Such an observation contradicts recent investments made by Nissan in order to establish itself as the largest automobile manufacturer of the country. So it would be interesting to analyze if there are differences in the interaction with suppliers among the Nissan's plants established in Mexico, and to study how this relation has evolved with time.

The experience of different countries has shown that productive agglomerations generate positive externalities (Barry et al. 2003). In Aguascalientes, the connection established between Tachi-S and Grupo MAEN is a significant example that confirms this argument. Nevertheless, specialization in attending only the needs of FDI-driving companies might create in local suppliers a degree of dependence that would be harmful for their future development. Thus, it is important for local companies to have their own vision about the future, oriented to the development of endogenous projects. Cuitlahuac Perez—CEO of MaindSteel and president of Grupo MAEN—is aware of the necessity to develop one's own research programs, not just because the relation with certain companies threatens dependency on them, but because it would be a step forward in the growth and development of local companies. Therefore, are the "combination of complementarity and the necessity of coping with dependency upon the business environment, the driving forces behind the development of such cooperation networks" (Irawati 2012:165).

To some extent, we can obtain an insight into the direction in which the Mexican automotive industry is moving, from the analysis of the available study programs and training of human resources carried out by Nissan. Taking a closer look at the programs mentioned before, we can observe that they appear to be more reactive, concentrating in solving current needs. In contrast, the introduction of structural innovations that address the development of the automotive industry, at least in some of its aspects, would require the introduction of completely new techniques (for instance, new production techniques, such as 3D printing with metals or other metal additive manufacturing techniques that provide several advantages, if compared with commonly used techniques). This observation highlights the need for public policies in education to consider future goals, that will laid in the ground of the automotive sector development. At the same time, it is an opportunity for Mexico to become an important player in the emerging and rapidly-developing innovation-based industry.

In addition, it is also important to note that the foreign investment policy of the Ministry of Economy in Mexico suggest that multinational companies have been endorsed the role of drivers of the Mexican automotive industry. However, this fact should not lead to a reduction of the role that Federal and State Governments play in the establishment of conditions for the proper integration of all the sectors involved in the development of the industry. In this sense, one of the observations made in our empirical research was that the government of Aguascalientes has been more reactive than proactive in designing policies oriented to a stronger degree of integration, as well as in addressing or shaping the sector in such a way that the experience obtained could be used for the establishment of projects intended to solve national problems, or that would involve resources or innovations available in Mexico. These actions are essential to avoid specialization degrees that could impede a timely response by the country's economy to challenges such as climate change and regulations associated with the reduction of human environmental impact, reflected in new priorities for developing "clean vehicles", etc.

With the idea of making the most of the demonstration effect of Japanese companies in the automotive sector in Aguascalientes, it is important to keep in mind that investments should not be an objective on their own, but should instead be the engine for the development of an innovative national industry, through strategies developed and enhanced in foreign countries to increase their efficiency. The huge advantage of Mexican companies, in this case, would be the knowledge of the national context and the possibility of using national technological developments. This path would imply the need for a broader vision in order to implement the more recent achievements of science—including those oriented to the replacement of the current vehicles using fossil fuels with the "clean" vehicles mentioned in the previous paragraph. Then, the benefits produced by the automotive industry must be reinvested and used as an engine for diversification of innovation industries that will form a basis for the economic prosperity of the country.

References

Altenburg, T. (2000). Linkages and spill-overs between transnational corporations and small and medium-sized enterprises in developing countries—opportunities and policies. *DIE-Deutsches Institut für Entwicklungspolitik*, 2000.

APEC Policy Support Unit. (2017, May). *Supporting industry promotion policies in APEC—Case study on Mexico*. Singapore: Asia-Pacific Economic Cooperation Secretariat. http://publications.apec.org/publication-detail.php?pub_id=1863. Accessed 19 July 2017.

Barry, F., Holger, G., & Strobl, E. (2003). Foreign direct investment, agglomeration and demonstration effects: An empirical investigation. *Review of World Economics/Weltwirtschaftliches Archiv, 139*, 583–600.

Cabrero Mendoza, E., & Orihuela, J. I. (2012). Construyendo los motores de la competitividad: Vinculación universidad-empresa en ciudades de México. In D. S. Cárdenas, M. E. Cabrero, & G. D. Arrellano (Eds.), *La difícil vinculación universidad-empresa en México*. México: CIDE.

CIMAT & IDEPMEX & CASCI Instituto de Desarrollo de Proveedores de México. (2016). *Factores que intervienen en la competitividad de la micro, pequeña y mediana industria en Aguascalientes: "un modelo de competitividad"*. http://fliphtml5.com/aedy/jbjd/basic. Accessed 13 June 2017.

CONACyT. (2014). *Agenda de Innovación de Aguascalientes*. 4.1. Agenda de área de especialización: automotriz y autopartes. http://www.agendasinnovacion.org/wp-content/uploads/2015/02/Agenda-Aguascalientes.pdf. Accessed 13 June 2017.

CONACyT. (2015a). Agenda de Innovación de Aguascalientes 2015, Mensaje de Elías Micha, Director Adjunto de Desarrollo Regional del Conacyt. http://www.agendasinnovacion.mx/wp-content/uploads/2015/02/Agenda-de-Innovaci%C3%B3n-de-Aguascalientes.pdf. Accessed 22 Aug 2016.

CONACyT. (2015b). Recibe Aguascalientes apoyos del Fondo Mixto y la Agenda Estatal de Innovación. Comunicado 13/15, February 24. http://www.conacyt.mx/index.php/comunicacion/comunicados-prensa/436-recibe-aguascalientes-apoyos-del-fondo-mixto-y-la-agenda-estatal-de-innovacion. Accessed 12 Apr 2016.

Corporativo Nissan. (n.d.). http://www.nissan.com.mx/corporativo/#nosotros. Accessed 11 Aug 2016.

CRÓNICA.com.mx. (2007, October 30). México pierde lugar en la industria de soporte: Japón. *Crónica,* http://www.cronica.com.mx/notas/2007/330484.html. Accessed 9 Sept 2016.

El Heraldo Aguascalientes. (2016a, August 7). *Apoyo primordial*. El Heraldo Aguascalientes, http://heraldo.mx/apoyo-primordial/. Accessed 23 Aug 2016.

El Heraldo Aguascalientes. (2016b, August 5). *CLT inauguró la Jornada Nacional de Alimentación*. El Heraldo Aguascalientes,. http://heraldo.mx/clt-inauguro-la-jornada-nacional-de-alimentacion/. Accessed 23 Aug 2016.

El Heraldo Aguascalientes. (2016c, April 15). *Crea Conalep la carrera Industria Automotriz*. El Heraldo Aguascalientes, http://heraldo.mx/crea-conalep-la-carrera-industria-automotriz/. Accessed 13 June 2017.

El Heraldo Aguascalientes. (2016d, April 14). *Presentará el Conalep la carrera Industria Automotriz*. El Heraldo Aguascalientes, http://heraldo.mx/presentara-el-conalep-la-carrera-industria-automotriz/. Accessed 13 June 2017.

El Universal. (2015, September 3). *Colocan primera piedra de COMPAS*. El Universal, http://www.eluniversal.com.mx/articulo/autopistas/2015/09/3/colocan-primera-piedra-del-complejo-compas-en-aguascalientes. Accessed 22 Aug 2016.

Gobierno del Estado de Aguascalientes. (2014). Parques industriales. http://www.parquesindustrialesags.org/parques-industriales/. Accessed 13 Jan 2017.

Gobierno del Estado de Aguascalientes. (2016). Rumbo y tendencias de Aguascalientes. http://aguascalientes.gob.mx/CEPLAP/SEIEG/cuadros/RUTA/RUTA.pdf. Accessed 22 Aug 2016.

González, O. (2016, December 9). Un programa para compartir el "expertise"automotriz de Aguascalientes al resto de estados. *Líder Empresarial*. http://www.liderempresarial.com/productividad/cittaa-el-proyecto-que-impulsara-el-sector-automotriz-local-para-fortalecer-la-industria-nacional/. Accessed 13 June 2017.

Grupo MAEN. (2016). http://www.grupomaen.mx/. Accessed 14 Aug 2016.

Hermosillo, H. (2017). Luego de 9 años, entra en funciones nuevo hospital Hidalgo. La Jornada Aguascalientes, December 15. http://www.lja.mx/2017/12/luego-9-anos-entra-en-funciones-nuevo-hospital-hidalgo. Accessed 8 June 2018.

INADEM. (n.d.). *Tutoriales de convocatorias*. https://tutoriales.inadem.gob.mx/mobile/index.php. Accessed 21 Aug 2016.

Indicadores Regionales de Actividad Económica. May 2017. (2017). https://www.banamex.com/analisis/revistas/IRAE/IRAEs2017.pdf. Accessed 12 June 2017.

INSA. (2016). Industria del Asiento Superior, S.A. de C.V. (INSA). http://www.tachi-s.mx/i/insa.htm. Accessed 19 Aug 2016.

Irawati, D. (2012). *Knowledge transfer in the automobile industry*. London/New York: Routledge.

JETRO Mexico. (2016). Automotive suppliers database. https://www.jetro.go.jp/mexico/indusporte.html. Accessed 14 June 2016.

Jordaan, J. A. (2009). *Foreign direct investment, agglomeration and externalities*. Farnham: Ashgate.

Kokko, A. (1994). Technology, market characteristics, and spillovers. *Journal of Development Economics, 43*, 279–293.

La Jornada Aguascalientes. (2015a, January 12). Aguascalientes: tercer lugar en Índice de Competitividad Estatal del IMCO. *La Jornada Aguascalientes.*, http://www.lja.mx/2015/01/aguascalientes-tercer-lugar-en-el-indice-de-competitividad-estatal-del-imco/. Accessed 23 Aug 2016.

La Jornada Aguascalientes. (2015b, August 3). Se realizó la graduación de la Escuela de Jatco. *La Jornada Aguascalientes.*, http://www.lja.mx/2015/08/se-realizo-la-graduacion-de-la-escuela-jatco/. Accessed 15 Apr 2016.

La Jornada Aguascalientes. (2016, August 10). Reconoce UAA respaldo y apoyo del Gobierno para su crecimiento. *La Jornada Aguascalientes.*, http://www.lja.mx/2016/08/reconoce-uaa-respaldo-apoyo-del-gobierno-crecimiento/. Accessed 23 Aug 2016.

Lara Enríquez, B. E. (2004). Encadenamientos productivos y promoción industrial en dos conglomerados automotrices. *Un acercamiento a las experiencias de Aguascalientes y Juárez (1990–2002)*. Thesis to obtain PhD in Social Sciences, El Colegio de la Frontera Norte.

Mexico Industry. (2016, January 31). *Sector Automotriz, motor de crecimiento*. Declaración de Eduardo Solís, Presidente Ejecutivo de la Asociación Mexicana de la Industria Automotriz (AMIA).

Moreno-Codina, T. (2015). Plan maestro del corredor logístico industrial automotriz del Bajío, *QUIVERA. Universidad Autónoma del Estado de México, 17*(1), 13–34.

NissanNews.com. (2014, July 25). *Datos Clave de la operación de Nissan en México*. http://nissannews.com/es-MX/nissan/mexico/releases/datos-clave-de-la-operacion-de-nissan-en-mexico. Accessed 22 Aug 2016.

NTR Zacatecas. (2016, June 8). *Crece el número de empleos registrados*. NTR Zacatecas, http://ntrzacatecas.com/2016/06/08/crece-el-numero-de-empleos-registrados/. Accessed 23 Aug 2016.

Okazaki, T. (2011, October 19). Expansión de empresas japonesas en el mundo y México en la Industria Automotriz, Presentación en el Club de Industriales, Cd. de México. https://www.jetro.go.jp/mexico/topics/20111020817-topics/Texto_Conferencia_DG_Okazaki_Club_Industriales_19oct11.pdf. Accessed 9 Sept 2016.

Romo Vázquez, A. (1994). La industrialización de la economía del estado de Aguascalientes (1940–1990). *Investigación y Ciencia, 11*, 42–50. http://www.uaa.mx/investigacion/revista/archivo/revista11/Articulo%207.pdf. Accessed 14 Jan 2017.

Saggi, K. (2002). Trade, foreign direct investment, and international technology transfer: A survey. *The World Bank Research Observer, 17*(2), 191–235.

Sánchez-Sellero, P., Rosell-Martinez, J., & García-Vázquez, J. M. (2014). Absorptive capacity from foreign direct investment in Spain manufacturing firms. *International Business Review, 23*, 429–439.

Secretaría de Economía (SE). (2013). Programa de Desarrollo Innovador 2013–2018, México. Accessed 15 June 2016.

SE/ProMéxico. (2015). *Diez Años 2005–2015 Acuerdo para el fortalecimiento de la Asociación Económica (AAE) entre México y Japón*.

UAA. (2016). Síntesis Histórica de la Universidad Autónoma de Aguascalientes. http://www.uaa.mx/nu/histog.php. Accessed 16 July 2016.

Interviews

Cedillo Díaz, L. General Director. Center for Competitiveness and Innovation of Aguascalientes state (CECOI), Aguascalientes. (2016, March 9). Personal interview.

Díaz, J.A. Director of Suppliers Development and Foreign Trade, Ministry of Economic Development of Aguascalientes State (SEDEC), Aguascalientes. (2016, February 16). Personal interview.

Gómez, A. CEO of Industrias DMU, Aguascalientes. (2016, May 6). Personal interview.

Pérez Abreu, L. Director of Executive Education, Center for the Development of the Automotive Industry in Mexico (CeDIAM), ITESM Campus Aguascalientes, Aguascalientes. (2016, March 8). Personal interview.

Pérez Cerros, C. CEO of MaindSteel and President of Grupo MAEN, Aguascalientes. (2016, March 8). Personal interview.

Ríos, A. Representative of JICA Mexico office. (2016, June 7). Personal interview.

Rodríguez, J. Regional Purchasing Manager, Tachi-S, Aguascalientes. (2016, June 9). Personal interview.

Sánchez, H. CEO of Metalistik, Aguascalientes. (2016a, May 5). Personal interview.

Sánchez, I. CEO of Servicios Técnicos Profesionales MARISA, S.A. de C.V., Aguascalientes. (2016b, May 6). Personal interview.

Zapiain Salinas, J. Head of the Department of Automotive Engineering, Universidad Autónoma de Aguascalientes (UAA), Aguascalientes. (2016, February 17). Personal interview.

Chapter 5
The Role of Public Policies in Attracting Japanese FDI in Mexico

Maria Guadalupe Lugo-Sanchez

Abstract With the debt crisis of the 1980s, an economic transition began, replacing import substitution industrialization, with the aim of adopting a series of structural reforms as a new model of economic growth. In order to obtain the benefits associated with investment, governments in developing countries relaxed their barriers to foreign investment flows and actively promote the attraction of FDI through the provision of subsidies and tax incentives. In the empirical literature, four factors are identified as determinants of the FDI location decision: regional demand, regional production costs, regional policies and the regional presence of agglomeration economies. Studies focused on public policies as a determinant factor for the location of FDI in developing countries are relatively scarce. This study is focused on the fiscal policies offered by the Bajio states, and their role in attracting Japanese foreign direct investment in the automotive industry.

Keywords Foreign direct investment · Public policies · Automotive industry · Mexico · Japan

5.1 Introduction

In the empirical and theoretical economic literature, Foreign Direct Investment (hereafter FDI) is regarded as a factor that stimulates economic growth. Many governments, from both developed and developing countries consider that FDI can benefit the host country through externalities or spillovers effects associated with this type of investment. Therefore, both in Mexico and in other Latin American countries, the attraction of FDI was considered to be one of the main factors to achieve economic

M. G. Lugo-Sanchez (✉)
Human Resources Department, University of Guadalajara, Zapopan, Mexico
e-mail: lupita.lugsan@gmail.com

M. Falck-Reyes, L. Guzman-Anaya (eds.), *Japanese Direct Investment in Mexico's Transport Equipment Sector*, New Frontiers in Regional Science: Asian Perspectives 22,
https://doi.org/10.1007/978-981-10-7718-0_5

growth and development. Consequently, governments implemented public policies in order to attract FDI offering investors tax incentives and subsidies since the 1980s.

After the debt crisis of 1980s the Mexico restructured its economy and policies, transitioning from a closed economic to an export – promoting industrial economy. The restrictions on FDI were relaxed, becoming the main source of financing in the early 90s (Gurria 1994); in the process of liberalization the Mexican government sought strategic partners in other economies[1] that allowed to stimulate trade. The signing of the North American Free Trade Agreement (NAFTA) was crucial to Mexico's economy for the promotion of manufacturing exports that were based on FDI; trade increased between Mexico and the United States as a result of NAFTA and investment flows to Mexico registered an upward trend with the arrival of manufacturing plants to the shared border of the two countries making Mexico an attractive destination for FDI.

In 1980, FDI flows to Mexico registered USD$ 2099 million; the effects of relaxation of barriers over the foreign direct investment are reflected at the end of the 1990s, when FDI flows reached US$ 18,315 million placing Mexico as the most important recipient of investment flows in Latin America. In 2013, the highest amount of FDI was recorded, at US$ 45,855 million (Fig. 5.1). At the beginning of the 1980s, FDI flows accounted for around 1% of the national GDP doubling in 1994, when NAFTA was signed (Fig. 5.2).

On the other hand, outflows of Japanese direct investment increased during the 1980s (Fig. 5.3) as a result of the Plaza accord of 1985 which led to an appreciation of the Japanese Yen and a consecutive loss of competitiveness of Japanese products in international markets, particularly in the United States, which led to seek for alternative markets for Japanese exports. NAFTA was one of the key factors that motivated Japan to sign an Economic Partnership Agreement with Mexico (the first EPA for Japan with a western country); the fact that Mexico had access to North American markets, among other reasons, encouraged Japan to sign the EPA in 2004.

Signing the EPA granted Japan access to Mexican markets enjoying preferential treatment, as well as the protection of Japanese investors in Mexico and, gained

Fig. 5.1 FDI flows to Mexico, in current prices and millions of USD (1980–2015)
Source: Author's own elaboration with data from UNCTAD

[1] Mexico has a network of 12 Free Trade Agreements with 46 countries, 32 Reciprocal Investment Promotion and Protection Agreements (RIPPAS) and 9 Trade Agreements (Economic Complementation and Partial Scope Agreements) within the framework of the Latin American Integration Association (ALADI). Secretariat of Economy.

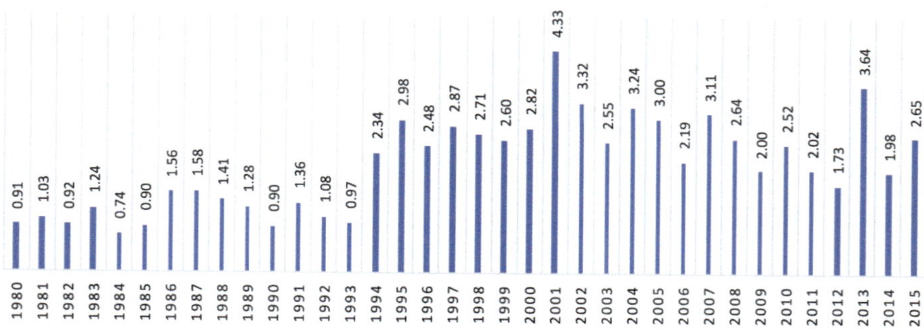

Fig. 5.2 FDI flows to Mexico as GDP percentage (1980–2015)
Source: Author's own elaboration with data from UNCTAD

Fig. 5.3 Total Japanese FDI flows, outward – millions of USD (1980–2015)
Source: Author's own elaboration with data from UNCTAD

access to participate in government bids. For Mexico, the EPA with Japan represents a strategy of diversification of trade and investment in Asia by attracting investment flows to different sectors, exporting Mexican products, importing products of technological nature under a preferential tariff, and, by gaining the benefits of bilateral cooperation like open markets, services and capital; it also represents an opportunity for Mexican suppliers to enter the Japanese productive chains.

Since its entry into force in 2005, FDI flows from Japan to Mexico have increased and are mainly destined to the automotive sector. In 2003, total Japanese FDI flows to Mexico were registered at US$ 139 million; by 2015 total flows were reported at US$ 1329 million.[2] The investment announced between 2003 and 2015 sums USD 22.95 billion[3]; FDI flows from Japan to Mexico are expected to increase, with the arrival of Toyota in 2016 to Celaya, Guanajuato. Toyota will produce the Tacoma model and a SUV, resulting in the creation of 2000 direct jobs. According to the Secretariat of Economy the production of automobiles in Mexico will extent up to

[2] Secretariat of Economy.

[3] The Financial Times.

5 million units in 2020,[4] positioning the country as one of the five major auto producers worldwide. For these reasons, understanding the factors that determine the location of new Japanese FDI becomes crucial for policy makers.

5.2 Literature Review

As mentioned previously by Jordaan (2009), regional demand, regional production costs, regional policies and regional presence of agglomeration economies are found in the literature as the four factors to locate FDI in a host country.

Hines (1996) evaluates the location of FDI investment based on a comparison of tax policies, and the study suggests that state taxes significantly influence the pattern of FDI in the United States. Also, Cheng and Kwan (2000) estimated the effects of the determinants of FDI and found that preferential policies, large regional markets and good infrastructure had positive effects, whereas wage cost had a negative effect in 29 Chinese regions for the period 1985 to 1995. Similarly, Cassidy and Andreosso-O'Callaghan (2006) found that the concentration of FDI in China was partially explained by the government policies that incentivized the location in coastal cities alongside the eastern seaboard, specifically where Special Economic Zones (SEZ) and economic and technological development zones were developed.

Lee et al. (2012) analyzed the location decision of Korean FDI in the United States and found that the location decision is more sensitively affected by the interstate difference in endowment conditions; in other words, business service and intermediate goods agglomeration are main determinants of FDI location.

Uwaoma (2012) conducts a study focusing on FDI and economic growth determinants for developing countries and the empirical evidence confirms that, changes in policies that affect inward FDI in a particular country affect inward FDI in surrounding countries. By lowering or eliminating investment costs (corporate taxes), a country can re-direct inward FDI from other host countries to itself.

Woodward (1992) analyzed the localization factors of Japanese FDI in the US during the 1980s and found that Japanese investors preferred states with strong markets and low unionization rates. Furthermore, unitary taxing methods were found to deter new start-ups and Japanese manufacturing plants favor states characterized by manufacturing agglomeration, low unemployment and low poverty rates and, where there is concentration of educated, productive workers. Similarly, Smith and Florida (1994) found that Japanese automotive related manufacturing establishments revealed a preference to locate in close proximity to Japanese automotive assemblers, with larger populations, a higher manufacturing density, a more educated workforce, and better transportation. Also, and contrasting with previous literature, the authors found also preference for locations with higher wages and higher concentration of minorities.

[4] http://www.elfinanciero.com.mx/empresas/toyota-invierte-mil-mdd-para-nueva-planta-en-celaya.html

In terms of public policies as a location determinant of Japanese FDI, according to Head et al. (1999), in 1980 governments from 19 states in US modified their policies in order to attract FDI from Japan, by opening foreign trade zones, establishing investment promotion offices in Japan and finally by eliminating taxing investors on a unitary basis. In their study, Head et al. (1999) assessed the influence of those state policies on the location decision of 760 Japanese manufacturing plants that arrived from 1980 to 1992 to US. Due to the fact that state promotional policies offset each other, the impact on the geographic distribution of Japanese investment appeared to be small. They conclude that in order to attract FDI, each country designs their own set of policies that may differ even at state levels. Also, Hyun (2008) studies the Japanese automotive industry in Europe, focusing in analyzing location decisions found that, for that particular case, during the decade of the 80s, location of Japanese firms was determined by trade barriers imposed in order to restrict Japanese production of automobiles in Europe.

Tokunaga et al. (2014) mention the importance of policies to improve industrial clusters efficiency. In their study of Japanese FDI in the manufacturing industry for the years 1985–2000, they also found horizontal and vertical agglomerations within the industries promote innovation and positive externalities. Successful government policies will need to promote and facilitate investments that improve preconditions for regional growth, design policies that attract the right type of FDI with respect to enhancing the potential scope of positive externalities within specific regional context, provide support to enhance the level absorptive capacity of Mexican firms and implement measures that support positive and curb detrimental regional and spatial externality effects from agglomeration and FDI. Such combination of policies will only be successful when the right combination of regional, multi-regional and federal funding and coordination is adopted (Jordaan 2009).

The growth of FDI flows has incited extensive research on the behavior of multinational firms and the localization factors associated with FDI. Little (1978) and Luger and Shetty (1985) are the first studies focusing on spatial characteristics and determinants of FDI. These studies found that higher wages discouraged FDI inflows from a region, while state government spending policies affected positively the location decision of foreign firms. The literature on spatial characteristics and other determinants of the location decision of FDI has primarily focused on developed countries, while the studies focusing on developing economies is still limited. One reason for the scarcity in research for developing countries, as Cassidy and Andreosso-O'Callaghan (2006) point out, is due to the difficulty in finding or generating reliable data at a regional, municipal or state level across countries.

Canfei (2006) finds that the acceleration of economic and political reforms in transitional economies has led to a surge of FDI inflows. Head et al. (1999) reported that regional corporate taxes, homogeneity in regional business taxes and regional labor subsidies are determinant for the selection of a location by an FDI project.

Other empirical results suggest that the characteristics that determine location for Japanese firms include market-size, potential labor market and wage level of the manufacturing sector. Also, the number of existing firms in an industry is significant for the location decision of Japanese firms (Guzman-Anaya 2015).

Regarding the effects of Japanese FDI as a source of economic growth, Fujita and Hill (1995) mention that Japanese FDI is characterized by production units, employing skilled workers with cooperative relations between management and the operating side, that translates into spills to the local economy, through human capital. Previous studies have shown that Japanese FDI contributes to economic growth, especially for Asian countries (Kojima 1985; Hahm and Heo 2008). Finally, Falck-Reyes (2012) finds that the arrival of FDI in the period following the signing of the AAEMJ improved the Mexican economy through increases in Mexican exports.

5.3 Japanese FDI in the Automotive Industry in Mexico

In recent years, the economic relationships between Mexico and Japan have strengthened, with the arrival of Japanese multinational companies of the automotive industry. The latter can be observed in the increasing bilateral trade flows (Lugo-Sanchez 2015) and the growing rates of Japanese FDI to Mexico, particularly after the entry into force of the EPA between these countries. The arrival of Japanese companies to Mexico has increased: from around 400 in 2009 to over 1000 in 2017 and, this growing trend of investment and business from Japan has not happened with any other country.

After the implementation of the new economic model during the decade of the 80s, and especially during this decade, FDI became relevant for the important role that played for the new development strategy for the country: as Dussel Peters (2000) points out, the depletion of other sources of external financing by the first half of the decade, such as agricultural and oil surplus and foreign debt was such, that not enough capital was available to cover the needs of Mexico's economy.

Historically, the manufacturing sector has been the main receptor of FDI: for the periods 1980–1988 the total share towards that sector recorded 66.34% and 12.4% was destined to the automotive sector. For the following years, 1989–1993, FDI flows grew at a slower pace, receiving 28.63%. The following period 1994–1999, was marked by the entry into force of NAFTA, and as expected, FDI flows started to increase; however, the period was also marked by a financial crisis in Asia, Russia and Brazil bringing international instability that affected FDI flows to Mexico (Dussel Peters 2000). For the latter period, the manufacturing sector was preferred over agricultural, followed by the sector of services. Particularly, the automotive sector benefited the most attracting 9.29% of the total FDI analyzed during those years.

Figure 5.4 shows FDI distribution by sectors in 2016: Manufactures captured 61.3% of total FDI received during that year, followed by other sectors and financial services.

The growth on the automobile sector as an effect of FDI was significant for Mexico resulting in strong forward and backward linkages in the economy (Kumaran 2008). The boost in production in the automotive industry can be thought as a result of the globalization, of the openness that increased the demand of products all over the world; consequently, the developing economies were presented with an oppor-

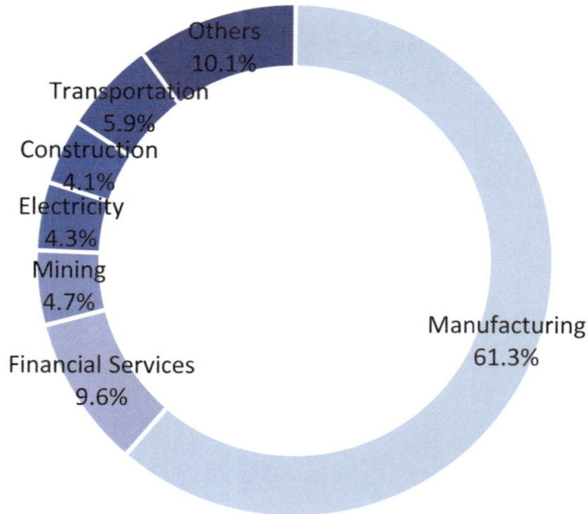

Fig. 5.4 FDI distribution by sectors in Mexico, 2016. In percentages
Source: Author's own elaboration with data from SE

tunity to participate in global markets. The benefits of hosting foreign companies (transfer of technology, improvement of existing industries, promotion of exports and employment) motivated the reform of existing policies to attract FDI.

The evolution of the automotive industry has been accompanied by the constant presence of the government, because it is considered as a key sector to achieve industrial development in Mexico. Therefore, since its origins the government has established different programs, known as "decrees" with the purpose of guiding the development of the industry. Even before the liberalization of the markets, those decrees regulated the sales and production, the number of companies participating in the industry, protectionism of the internal market and restriction to foreign investment as well as the percentage of local contents per unit of production (Brown Grossman 1999).

The Mexican automotive and auto parts industry has been able to position the country as the fourth largest exporter and the seventh largest producer in the world. The sector has received around USD$ 23.2 trillion in new investment from 2013 to date. During 2013, Mexico ranked 8th place among the largest vehicle manufacturers, with 3.07 million units manufactured in 19 of the world's leading car companies established along the 14 states of the country, displacing France and Spain, two countries with a long tradition in the automotive sector. The importance of the contribution of the sector can be reflected in the country's main economic indicators: by 2013 represented 2% share of total GDP, 15% of manufacturing production, 9% of FDI and 30% of total exports. The main destination for vehicle exports is North America (United States and Canada), which accounts for 76.6% of domestic production, followed by Latin America (12.7%), Europe (5.9%) and Asia (2.8%). Within the manufacturing industry, the automotive sector registers the highest paid wages with a 35% increase for the period 2006–2013 (ProMéxico 2014; 2015).

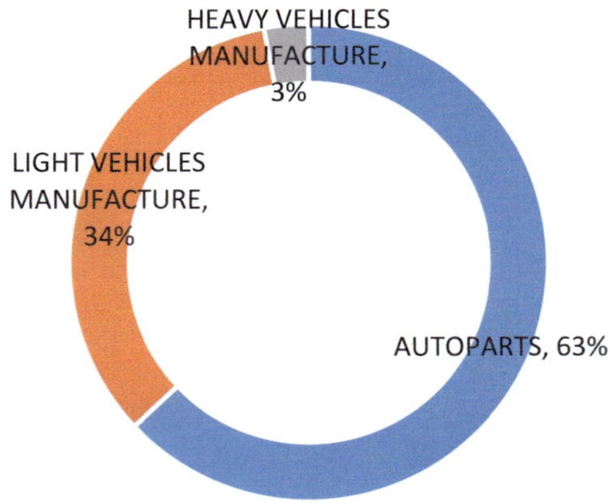

Fig. 5.5 FDI distribution in Mexico's automotive sector, 2016. In percentages
Source: Author's own elaboration with data from SE

FDI flows are distributed in the automotive sector as follows: 3% is destined to the production of heavy vehicles; 34% to the manufacture of light vehicles, and 63% is directed towards the production of auto parts (Fig. 5.5), being United States the country with larger investment flows to Mexico in the sector with 53.9% of participation for the years 1999–2016, followed by Japan, with 14.6% of participation. Germany's share of participation in the sector accounts for 11%, while the Netherlands and Spain percentage reaches 4.7 and 3.4 percentage respectively. The closeness and historical commercial ties have favored the investment flows between Mexico and United States (Fig. 5.6).

Of the total FDI received by Mexico from developed economies, Japan became the fifth largest country in 2005, preceded by investment from the United States, Spain, the Netherlands, the United Kingdom and Germany (Dussel Peters et al. 2007).

Japanese FDI in Mexico has concentrated mainly in the manufacturing industry, with a greater participation in the automotive and electronics sector with 76.72%. Figure 5.7 shows JFDI vs Total FDI flows to Mexico.The signing of NAFTA in the mid-1990s attracted the attention of Japanese investors, who had begun to move their production from the United States to the northern states of Mexico. Nissan's arrival in the Bajio region of Mexico attracted more investment to the area, with the establishment of its two plants in Aguascalientes and Morelos, beginning the trend of location for Japanese FDI.

In addition to human capital development and participation in the country's macroeconomic variables, the presence of Japanese FDI in the automotive sector in the manufacturing industry contributes to the establishment of different Information Technology (IT) centers, in particular the Technological Development Center of Nissan, the first of its kind, employing 366 engineers of local origin, whose main objective is the development of technologies to reduce pollutant emissions, and to collaborate closely with similar centers located in United States and Brazil.

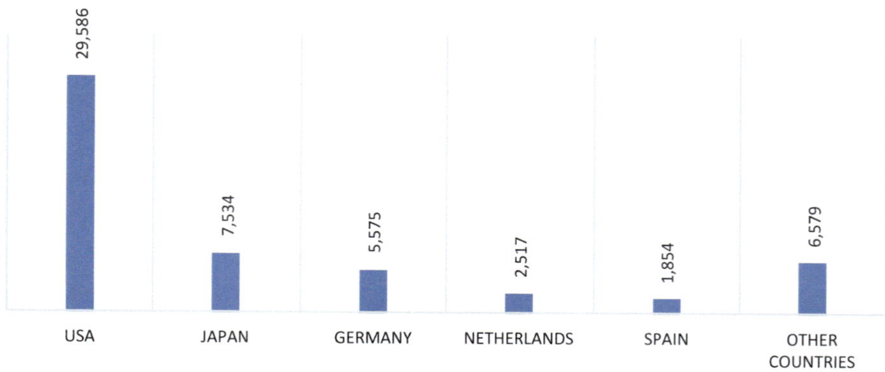

Fig. 5.6 FDI flows to Mexico's automotive sector by country of origin, 2016. In millions of USD
Source: Author's own elaboration with data from SE

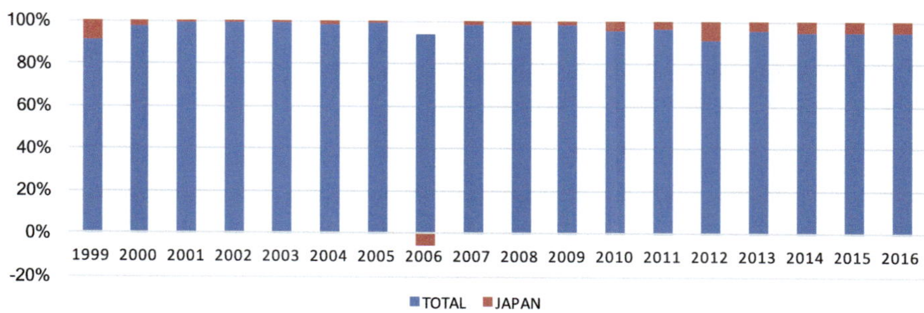

Fig. 5.7 Percentage of total FDI vs Japanese FDI flows to Mexico, (1999–2016)
Source: Author's own elaboration with data from SE

5.4 Public Policies, the States and Their Role in Attracting Japanese FDI

In addition to the plants situated in the northern border states, Japanese FDI is concentrated in the western region of the country, preferring the states of Guanajuato, Aguascalientes and Queretaro (where Mazda, Honda, Toyota and Nissan plants are located, see Fig. 5.8), an area with strong presence of companies in the automotive sector, characterized by other factors such as the specialization of the labor force as well as the road and rail infrastructure that facilitates the access of the finished products to the North American market and that eases distribution to South America. The investment in the state of Jalisco stands out for the establishment of the Honda plant in El Salto. Thus, the investment concentrated in the states of the Bajio region represents approximately 51% of the total Japanese FDI in the country. The Bajio is the most dynamic region in terms of Japanese FDI, which has quintupled in the last 4

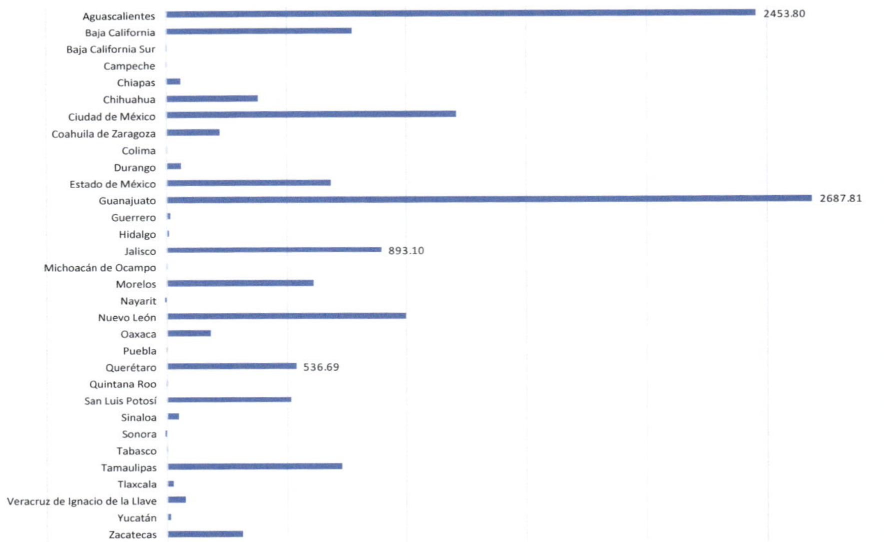

Fig. 5.8 Japanese FDI received by state, in millions of USD (1999–2016)
Source: Author's own elaboration with data from SE

years. This investment has had a positive impact on employment generation, exports and on labor training (Falck-Reyes 2012). Japanese investment has had positive impacts over employment even before the Partnership Agreement was signed. In fact, according to a study carried out by JETRO-Mexico (2004), 3 out of 100 formal jobs are generated by companies of Japanese origin established in Mexico.

During the period 1999 to 2016, Japanese FDI was distributed geographically as follows: Guanajuato had been the main recipient with USD$ 2687 million, followed by the States of Aguascalientes (USD$ 2453 millions), Jalisco (USD$ 893 millions) and Queretaro (USD$ 536 millions) (Fig. 5.8).

In contrast, Figure 5.9 shows the number of current fiscal incentives designed to attract FDI in selected states; from the states of interest, Aguascalientes reports that has introduced 11 incentives, Guanajuato 10, Jalisco 9 and Queretaro only 4 fiscal incentives. Figure 5.9 also shows a low correlation between states with low number of policies to attract investment and Japanese investment when compared with Fig. 5.8. The states with the higher numbers of policies are located on the South East and Northern part of the country and, when compared with the numbers on Fig. 5.8, the states in those regions receive the lowest flows of FDI from Japan; perhaps a reflection of the intensive efforts of the government to promote further advance less benefited local economies.

State governments offer incentives to new investors under confidential negotiations with representatives of both parties (companies and government. According to data from the state secretariats for economic development, the fiscal incentive more frequently employed by the states is the temporary exemption or reduction of payroll taxes and, special incentives for research and development (used by 24 states)

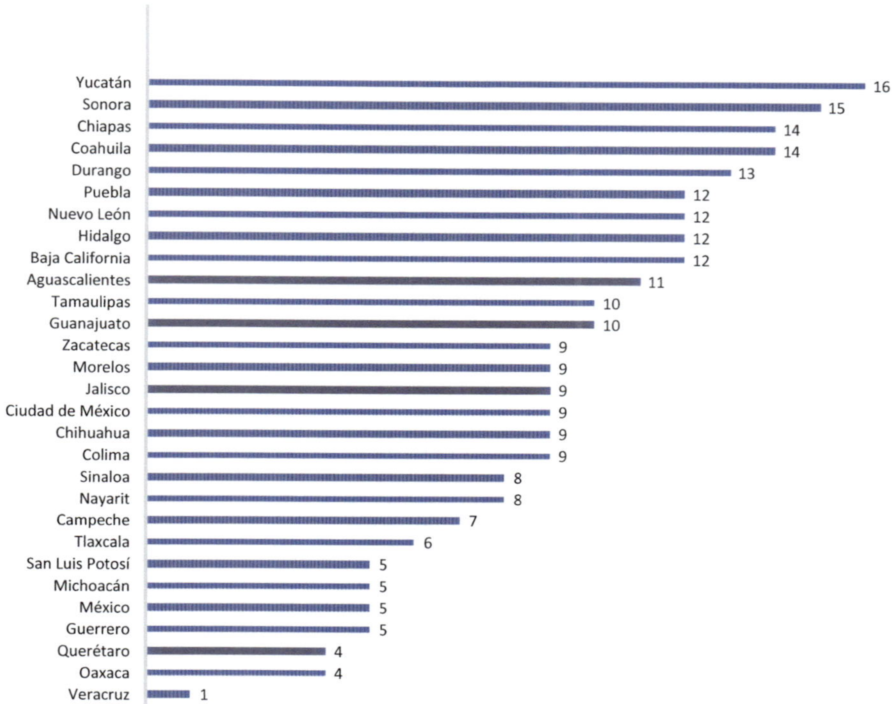

Fig. 5.9 Number of fiscal incentives for FDI attraction offered by state and municipality, 2015
Source: Author's own elaboration with data from State Governments and/or State Secretariats of Economic Development, 2015

followed by incentives related to the exemption of state taxes and duties, of payments related to procedures to register the activities and operations of the company, exemption or reduction of property taxes, and incentives to promote projects outside metropolitan areas (used by 22 states). Table 5.1 depicts the nature of the incentives and the number of states applying the incentives.

Guanajuato, the state with higher JFDI flows in the automotive industry, actively supports the establishment of new companies, through the design of fiscal policy incentives accompanied by the improvement of industrial, commercial and services infrastructure in order to create new and permanent jobs and to benefit municipalities or regions through economic spillovers brought by FDI.

As a strategy to achieve economic development in Guanajuato, FDI policies are designed to foster GDP through five fundamental objectives: (a) generation of new jobs and FDI attraction (b) establishment and execution of investment projects of high added value, and high technological content, and to promote import substitution; (c) strengthening of productive chains (and diversification within the local industry); (d) promotion of strategic projects of industrial infrastructure; and (e) specialization and development of human capital.

Table 5.1 Fiscal incentives for FDI attraction per state and municipalities in Mexico, 2015

Fiscal incentives for investment in the Mexican states (and municipalities) 2015			
Type of incentive	Number of states applying the incentive	Type of incentive	Number of states applying the incentive
Temporary exemption or reduction of Payroll Tax (ISN)	24	Exemption or reduction of fees for the issuance of a Construction Permit	16
Special incentives for research and development projects	24	Exemption or reduction of the Property Transfer Tax	14
Temporary exemption or reduction of State Taxes and Duties	22	Temporary exemption or reduction of the Tax on Property or Use of Motor Vehicles	14
Exemption or reduction on the payment of duties related to the Public Registry of Property and Trade	22	Exemption or reduction of fees related with the revision of blueprints	12
Temporary exemption or reduction on the Property Tax	22	Exemption or reduction of real estate appraisal costs	12
Special incentives for projects outside the metropolitan area	22	Exemption or reduction on the payment of duties for connection to the potable water net and sewerage	9
Temporary exemption or reduction of the payment for the Land use License	18	Temporary exemption or reduction on the payment of public lighting duties	7
Exemption or reduction of the Real Estate Acquisition Tax	18	Exemption or reduction of the payment of fees related to the registration and issuance of plates, sticker and the Vehicle License	7

Source: Author's own elaboration with data from State Governments and/or State Secretariats of Economic Development, 2015

Fiscal incentives are subjected to project evaluation, and will be granted to those projects designed to reach the fundamental objectives aforementioned. States governments are not obligated to grant incentives: as an instrument of economic promotion, fiscal incentives are subjected to availability and budget considerations. Each investment project has particularities and therefore, the negotiations to grant the incentives cannot follow the same rigid parameters. Those projects that will generate largest spillovers, or a significant amount of new jobs, or that aid the incursion of local companies to productive chains will be prioritized.

The incentives to encourage the establishment of productive investment can be oriented to the initial installation and operations of the company; to the process of legal constitution of the company, and to train human resources, etcetera. The monetary amount to be granted is calculated according to certain parameters such as the number of new jobs, or the investment volume and, the economic activity (Table 5.2).

Table 5.2 Fiscal incentives by state in the Bajio Region

	Bajio States			
	Aguascalientes	Guanajuato	Jalisco	Querétaro
Fiscal incentives				
1 Temporary exemption or reduction of State Taxes and Duties	No	Yes	Yes	No
2. Temporary exemption or reduction of Payroll Tax (ISN)	Yes	Yes	Yes	No
3. Temporary exemption or reduction of the payment for the Land use License	Yes	Yes	Yes	Yes
4. Exemption or reduction of fees related with the revision of blueprints	Yes	No	No	No
5. Exemption or reduction of real estate appraisal costs	Yes	Yes	No	No
6. Exemption or reduction of the Property Transfer Tax	No	No	No	Yes
7. Exemption or reduction of the Real Estate Acquisition Tax	Yes	No	No	No
8. Exemption or reduction on the payment of duties related to the Public Registry of Property and Trade	Yes	Yes	Yes	Yes
9. Temporary exemption or reduction on the Property Tax	Yes	Yes	Yes	No
10. Exemption or reduction of fees for the issuance of a Construction Permit	No	No	No	No
11. Exemption or reduction on the payment of duties for connection to the potable water net and sewerage	No	No	No	No
12. Temporary exemption or reduction on the payment of public lighting duties	No	No	No	No
13. Temporary exemption or reduction of the Tax on Property or Use of Motor Vehicles	Yes	Yes	Yes	Yes
14. Exemption or reduction of the payment of fees related to the registration and issuance of plates, sticker and the Vehicle License	Yes	Yes	Yes	No
15. Special incentives for research and development projects	Yes	Yes	Yes	No
16. Special incentives for projects outside the metropolitan area	Yes	Yes	Yes	No
Total	**11**	**10**	**9**	**4**

Source: Author's own elaboration with data from State Governments and/or State Secretariats of Economic Development, 2015

The Government of Guanajuato publishes a document through the Secretariat of Economy of the state, containing the requirements that investors must meet in order to apply for fiscal incentives; the document is printed in the official newspaper of the state Government.

The Government of Guanajuato divides the state in three different zones, and each municipality is located within one of the zones; the least developed zones receive higher percentages of economic incentives.

Guanajuato competes against Aguascalientes, Jalisco, Queretaro and San Luis Potosi for FDI. But perhaps the hardest race for this type of investment occurs within the state: with six industrial corridors[5] located along the municipalities where Japanese companies operate, negotiators have to compete not only with other municipalities, but with other states as well.

The government of Aguascalientes, on the other hand, besides the fiscal incentives to attract FDI, aims to improve the infrastructure available to promote the arrival of new centers of applied research and technological development for the industries and companies operating in the state. The administration is encouraging the promotion and consolidation of existing industrial parks such as TECNOPOLO, as well as the creation of another High Technology Industrial Park focused on hosting new research centers.

A new Research and Technological Innovation Park will also be developed with the capacity and infrastructure to attract more investment to promote applied research and innovation, link research to the needs of the market and business, and build high-level intellectual capital, facilitating the transfer of knowledge to generate new products and businesses. Policy design is focused on the improvement of financial instruments, tax incentives and risk capital to support innovation and technological development in companies in the region.

Queretaro has a special legislation for industrial investors. Entrepreneurs seeking to locate in geographical zones outside the metropolitan area can benefit from tax benefits, according to indicators of the state's fiscal incentives. When the companies assign part of their operating expenses to research and technological and scientific development, as well as when they make investments to solve problems of environmental pollution in the field of recycling, treatment and construction of domestic and industrial waste, also receive fiscal benefits. Even though Queretaro is the state with the least amount of fiscal incentives offered, the government announced that it is not contemplating the creation of new policies to attract investment from Asia and Europe, nor the reduction of its taxes. The administration considers the existing fiscal incentives to be fair and not excessive, and the strategy to promote local industry

[5] Economic corridors in Guanajuato with presence of companies in the automotive industry:

1. Corredor Silao – San Felipe – Pueblos del Rincon.
2. Corredor de la Carretera Federal 57.
3. Corredor de la Carretera Federal 45.
4. Corredor Celaya – Acambaro.
5. Corredor Irapuato – Penjamo.
6. Corredor San Miguel de Allende – Dolores Hidalgo – Guanajuato.

is through training human resources to meet the needs of existing companies. The administration plans to strengthen small and medium local companies through training programs in order to link them into higher productive chains. Perhaps the only exception is the promotion of a policy to grant fiscal incentives on payroll tax to companies that hire deported nationals, as a response to the migratory policies supported by Donald Trump's administration. Finally, Queretaro seems to be steering towards a different industry: on March of 2016 a plan was announced to develop an Aerospace Cluster. The project consists in four milestones that comprise 15 strategic projects of development and promotion to that particular sector in the state, regarding to research, development and design of products, as well as processes and services of the industry; including manufacture of small aircraft, among others.

Jalisco stated that the promotion of productive investment must be a priority for the public administration of the different entities at municipal and state level, and that all their actions should be aimed at attracting and consolidating business projects which should be selected through a previous analysis (that includes a systematic study of the markets and economic behavior) to ensure that the projects boost the productive specialization of a given geographic area, and improve its competitive position. Investment acquisition actions include exploration of specific projects, constitution and equipment of territorial reserves for productive purposes, provision of land for the location of economic units, provision of services infrastructure and business logistics, facilitation of access to financing and the conclusion of alliances and co-investments between productive agents.

The consolidation of business projects includes the granting of incentives for the establishment of new companies or the expansion of existing ones, the accompaniment and the subscription or renegotiation of conditions for the retention or reconversion of work centers.

Next, it's pertinent to review the state Competitiveness Index (SCI) of 2016 for the region of interest. The SCI measures the ability of the states to attract and retain talent and investments. A competitive state is one that is consistently attractive to talent and investment, which translates into greater productivity and well-being for its habitants.

In 2016 Aguascalientes ranked as the second most competitive state due to an adequate administration of its government, the development of its innovative potential and the sustainable management of its natural resources.

Queretaro ranked fifth most competitive state, derived in part from the stimulus to innovation. In 2014 was the second state with the largest number of companies and scientific and technological institutions, the third with more academic researchers and patents and the ninth with greater economic complexity in the innovation sectors. Jalisco ranked 8th place while Guanajuato was registered in the 18th position.

The SCI is comprised of ten categories. Each state is evaluated within each of those categories according to their achievements every year (Table 5.3). The numbers in green denote the place that the state ranked per category, that are above the national average. The numbers in red represent the place they occupy, and show that the state is below the national average.

Table 5.3 Ranking of the Bajio states per competitiveness index

2014 Ranking						
	Index	Description	Aguascalientes	Guanajuato	Jalisco	Queretaro
1	Reliable and objective right system	Measures the public and legal security environment in the states of the country	8	7	23	13
2	Sustainable management of the environment	Measures the capacity of the States to manage natural resources and their environment in a sustainable and responsible manner	2	19	3	12
3	Inclusive, prepared and healthy society	Measures the quality of life of the habitants through three areas: inclusion, education and health	5	24	11	6
4	Stable and functional political system	Capability of stable and functional state systems	22	19	18	24
5	Efficient and effective government	Measures how governments are able to positively influence the competitiveness of their states	2	22	5	3
6	Efficient Factor Market	Measures the productivity of workers and other essential characteristics of employment	5	22	21	10
7	Stable economy	Measures the main characteristics of the state economies, as well as the credit situation for companies and families	8	13	5	6
8	World-Class Precursor Sectors	Measures the financial, telecommunications and transport sectors	8	24	3	20
9	Harnessing international relations	Measures the extent to which states capitalize on their relationship with the outside world to raise their competitiveness	9	14	7	13
10	Innovation of the economic sectors	Measures the ability of states to successfully compete in the economy, particularly in high-value-added, knowledge-intensive and state-of-the-art sectors	3	13	12	1

Source: Author's own elaboration with data from Mexican Institute for Competitiveness, 2016

The Table 5.3 shows that Aguascalientes is the state that has a more favorable environment for investment, followed by Queretaro, Jalisco and Guanajuato.

Even though Guanajuato is the state that receives larger flows of JFDI, is ranked last among the Bajio states by the study conducted by the Mexican Institute for Competitiveness, which may indicate that the existence of a cluster plays a greater part over the attraction of JFDI.

Have the expected results been achieved in terms of economic growth? Figure 5.10 shows the growth rate of the GDP of the Bajio States compared to the growth rate of Mexico. First, an upward trend can be observed after 2005, following the entry into force of the economic partnership agreement between Mexico and Japan, where Aguascalientes occupies the first place in growth. Guanajuato's trend is also noticeable, surpassing the national GDP growth in 2006. After the financial crisis of 2009, we can observe that Queretaro led in terms of growth until 2013. Aguascalientes registered the highest growth rate with 11.18% in 2014. In general, the Bajio states remained above national growth for the period 2004–2015 (Fig. 5.11).

In the growth rate analysis of the manufacturing sector for the Bajio states, Queretaro takes the lead for the entire period, even after the crisis of 2009. Again, the Bajio states show a growth rate above the national growth rate for this sector (Fig. 5.12).

In terms of unemployment rates, Jalisco has the lowest of the Bajio States, and fluctuates around the national unemployment line. Guanajuato has the second lowest unemployment rates of the Bajio states, while Aguascalientes records the highest unemployment rates and the lowest sectorial growth.

The data analyzed offers a perspective of the behavior of the Bajio states in terms of economic growth, employment and FDI attraction. However is difficult to relate the effects of the fiscal policies over the location decision of Japanese companies at a local level.

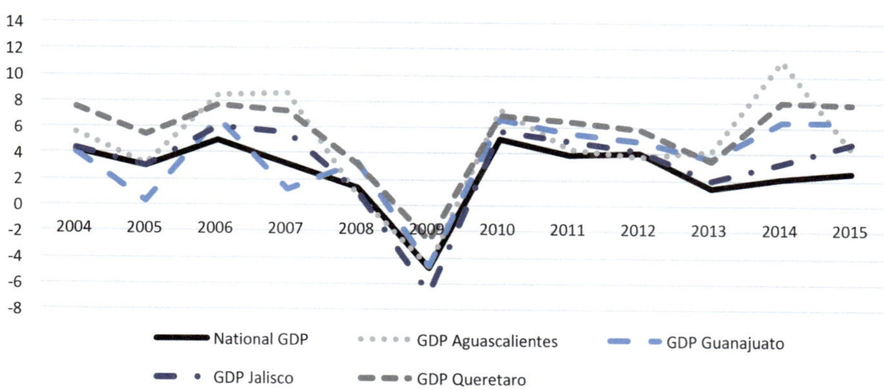

Fig. 5.10 National growth rate, compared to Bajio states growth rate. 2004–2015. In percentages
Source: Author's own elaboration with data from INEGI

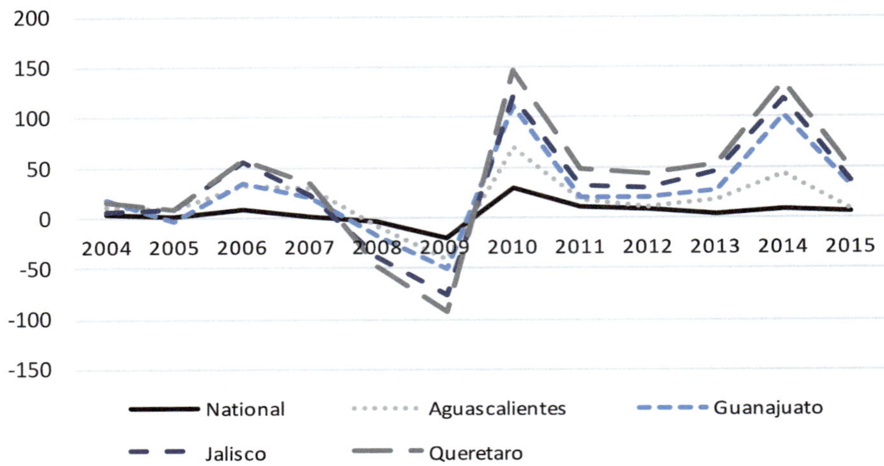

Fig. 5.11 National manufacturing sector growth rate, compared to Bajio states growth rate. 2004–2015. In percentages
Source: Author's own elaboration with data from INEGI

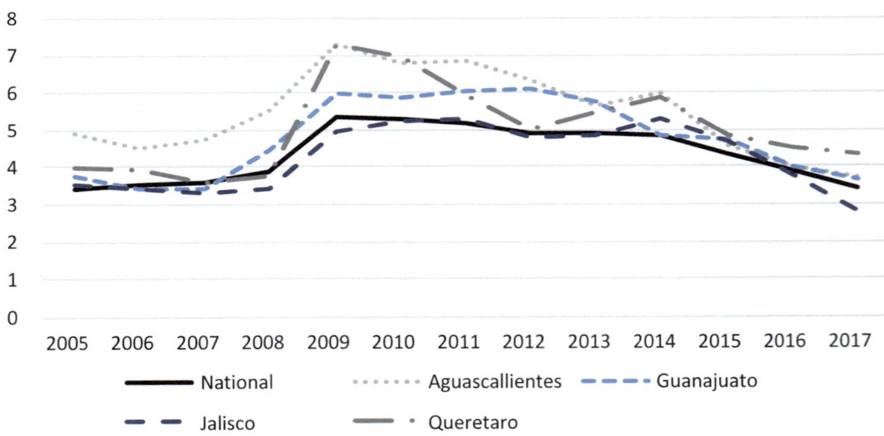

Fig. 5.12 Unemployment rate for Bajio states. 2004–2015. In percentages
Source: Author's own elaboration with data from INEGI

A study conducted during May of 2015 on a sample of 19 Japanese companies of the automotive sector in the Bajio region revealed that eight companies received fiscal incentives from the government,[6] and the nature of the incentives were: Government financing to acquire land and other benefits, such as rent payments and human resources; government program that granted funds that were linked to the

[6] Due to the nature of the negotiations, representatives of the companies that were interviewed were not allowed to disclose the terms or details of negotiations. In other cases, the interviewee ignored the details of the negotiation for not being present during that process.

amount to be invested and to hiring Mexican workforce and, fiscal incentives during the acquisition of land and assets. Those incentives were mentioned by the companies as factors to determine their location preference at a local level. However, during the interviews, it was clear that the companies have considered Mexico over other countries, due to factors like regional production costs, regional demand presence of Japanese companies in the industry, existing infrastructure and qualified labor force.

5.5 Conclusions

Mexico has successfully built a solid automotive supply network that facilitates the operation logistics of the companies in the automotive industry and offers highly qualified human resources. Japan on the other hand has capital, advanced managerial skills and developed scientific and technological resources; these differences make them complementary economies. Mexico ranks in 8th place as an attractive destination for investment according to the 2016 UNCTAD business survey. Not only is one of the leading countries in advanced manufactures exports, but also offers a stable macroeconomic environment and legal protection to investment.

The arrival of Nissan to Aguascalientes in 1960s marked the beginning of regional industrial development that decades later would evolve into an important automotive cluster for the Bajio region. For the last four decades, Nissan has created a strong distribution, supply and cooperation network, between government and academic researchers to further improve their position as one of the leading companies in the industry.

The Bajio region has benefited from the arrival of Japanese FDI, and local governments of the different states have actively worked towards the promotion of their entities through fiscal incentives. Those incentives were a recognized as a key factor to determine location preference for companies, across states and municipalities. However, for the case of Japanese FDI regional demand, regional production costs, and regional presence of agglomeration economies play a bigger role in attracting investment flows, according to the research conducted with Japanese companies.

In addition to fiscal policies, governments are faced with the challenge of responding to demands of Japanese companies operating in the Bajio states on the need for local producers and skilled labor on the one hand; on the other hand, to the greater challenge of attaining sustainable economic development for the region.

Aguascalientes is responding by promoting the interest in technology at all academic levels, implementing workshops and laboratories with basic principles of Mechatronics in the schools, to lead the new generations to attain higher education in high technology programs. The government understands the imperative necessity to reinforce English as a second language, as well as academic programs in computer science and mathematics. The state supports the universities that participate in the triple helix dynamics, and support the creation of new centers of research and technological development, and understands the importance of adapting the existing academic programs to satisfy the demand of the companies in the automotive industry.

In terms of competitiveness, according to the National Institute of Statistics and Geography (INEGI), the Mexican Institute for Competitiveness, among other national organizations, Queretaro occupies the first places in the growth of GDP in the country, with positive trends in this area thanks to its scientific and technological development, the productive link between academia and the industrial sector, and the growing foreign direct investment that generates more jobs, boosting the domestic market .

Competition for FDI between states can lead to a deterioration of the finances of the local governments, so the authorities in charge of the public finances of the country encourage the administrations of the states involved to coordinate local efforts to define and limit the incentives, to avoid cannibalization of investment between the states.

Globally, the trend on policies is to continue to promote investment liberalization; still, an important concern for policymakers is the gap between productive investment and income generation that has repercussions on sustainable economic development.

References

Brown Grossman, F. (1999). *La industria de autopartes mexicana: Reestructuración reciente y perspectivas*. División de desarrollo productivo y empresarial de la comisión económica para América Latina y el Caribe centro internacional de investigación para el desarrollo.

Canfei, H. (2006). Regional descentralisation and location of foreign direct investment in China. *Post-Communist Economies, 18*, 33–50.

Cassidy, J., & Andreosso-O'Callaghan, B. (2006). Spatial determinants of Japanese FDI in China. *Japan and the World Economy, 18*(4), 512–527.

Cheng, L. K., & Kwan, Y. K. (2000). What are the determinants of the location of foreign direct investment? The Chinese experience. *Journal of International Economics, 51*(2), 379–400.

Dussel Peters, E. (2000). *La inversión extranjera en México*. Serie Desarrollo Productivo (pp. 1–103).

Dussel Peters, E., Galindo Paliza, L., Loria, E., & Mortimore, M. (2007). *La inversión extranjera directa en México: desempeño y potencial*. México: Siglo veintiuno editores.

Falck-Reyes, M. (2012). Japanese foreign direct investment in Mexico and the impact of the global crisis. *Journal of Globalization Competitiveness and Governability, 6*(1), 36–54.

Fujita, K., & Hill, R. (1995). Global toyotaism and local development international. *Journal of Urban and Regional Research, 19*(1), 7–22.

Gurria, J. (1994). Flujos de capital: el caso de México. *Serie Financiamiento del Desarrollo CEPAL, 27*.

Guzman-Anaya, L. (2015). Localization factors from Japanese firms in automotive- related industries in Mexico. *Procedia Economics and Finance, 30*(2015), 265–270.

Hahm, S., & Heo, U. (2008). U.S. and the Japanese foreign direct investment in East Asia: A comparative analysis. *The Policy Studies Journal, 36*(6), 119–133.

Head, C., Ries, J. C., & Swenson, D. L. (1999). Attracting foreign manufacturing: Investment promotion and agglomeration. *Regional Science and Urban Economics, 29*(2), 197–218.

Hines, J. (1996). Altered states: Taxes and the location of foreign direct investment in America. *The American Economic Review, 86*(5), 1076–1094.

Hyun, J. (2008). A comparative analysis of transplants and industrial location of Japanese and Korean automotive industries in Europe. *International Journal of Business, 13*, 216–238.

IMCO. Un puente entre dos Méxicos. (2016). *Índice de Competitividad Estatal.*

JETRO-México. (2004). *Relaciones Económicas México-Japón*. México City: JETRO México.

Jordaan, J. (2009). *Foreign direct investment, agglomeration and externalities: Empirical evidence from Mexican manufacturing industries* (pp. 1–211). London/New York: Routledge.

Kojima, K. (1985). Japanese and American direct investment in Asia: A comparative analysis. *Hitotsubashi Journal of Economics, 25*, 1–20.

Kumaran, G. (2008). Role of multinational corporations in automobile industries: A comparative study between India and Mexico. *PORTES, revista mexicana de estudios sobre la Cuenca del Pacífico, 2*(3), 131–163.

Lee, K., Hwang, S., & Lee, M. (2012). Agglomeration economies and location choice of Korean manufacturers within the United States. *Applied Economics, 44*(2), 189–200.

Little, J. (1978, July/August de). Location decisions of foreign direct investors in the United States. *New England Economic Review, 18*, 43–63.

Luger, M., & Shetty, S. (1985). Determinants of foreign plant start-ups in the United States: Lessons for policymakers in the southeast. *Vanderbilt Journal of Transnational Law, 18*(2), 223–245.

Lugo-Sanchez, M. G. (2015). *Economic partnership agreement Mexico – Japan: Trade creation or trade diversion*. Revista Green Paper, 1–25.

ProMéxico. (2014). *Automotive industry*. México, D.F.: ProMéxico.

ProMéxico. (2015). *The Mexican automotive industry: Leading the world*. México, D.F.: ProMéxico.

Smith, D., & Florida, R. (1994). Agglomeration and industrial location: An econometric analysis of Japanese-affiliated manufacturing establishments in automotive-related industries. *Journal of Urban Economics, 36*(1), 23–41.

Tokunaga, S., Kageyama, M., Akune, Y., & Nakamura, R. (2014). Empirical analysis of agglomeration economies in the Japanese assembly type manufacturing industry for 1985–2000: Using agglomeration and coagglomeration indices. *Review of Urban and Regional Development Studies, 26*, 57–81.

Uwaoma, G. (2012). Essays on spatial analysis of foreign direct investment and economic growth determinants in developing countries. *Dissertations, 33*, 1–24.

Woodward, D. (1992). Locational determinants of Japanese manufacturing start- ups in the United States. *Southern Economic Journal, 58*(3), 690–708.

Chapter 6
The Impact of Japanese Training Programs on Local Automotive Suppliers' Productivity in Mexico's State of Guanajuato

Leo Guzman-Anaya

Abstract The present chapter studies the role of Training Programs (TPs) as mechanisms for technological and knowledge transfer to local firms and the productivity enhancements achieved from these processes. Specifically, the analysis is centered on the "Project for Automotive Supply Chain Development in Mexico" that was promoted between Japanese and Mexican development agencies and the state governments of Guanajuato, Queretaro and Nuevo Leon. The overall results from the project indicate positive effects from the TPs on the productivity of local firms. Similar findings are reported for the case of Guanajuato, where local participating firms in the TPs experienced an effective technological and knowledge transfer of Japanese style management and production methods with significant improvements on productivity and quality indicators.

Keywords Training programs · Technological and knowledge transfer · Productivity spillovers

6.1 Introduction

In the field of international development cooperation, training programs (TPs) have served as mechanisms to transfer technology and knowledge from developed to developing countries with an expected impact on the capacities of local workforces and productivity of local firms. The Japanese International Cooperation Agency (JICA) is an organization offering these types of programs to developing countries since joining the Colombo Plan in 1954. During the last 60 years more than 310,000 people from 198 countries have been trained through one of JICA's programs in a variety of areas such as governance, urban and regional development, health and medicine, education, environment management, peacebuilding and social security,

L. Guzman-Anaya (✉)
Human Resources Department, University of Guadalajara, Zapopan, Mexico
e-mail: leo.guzman8@gmail.com

M. Falck-Reyes, L. Guzman-Anaya (eds.), *Japanese Direct Investment in Mexico's Transport Equipment Sector*, New Frontiers in Regional Science: Asian Perspectives 22,
https://doi.org/10.1007/978-981-10-7718-0_6

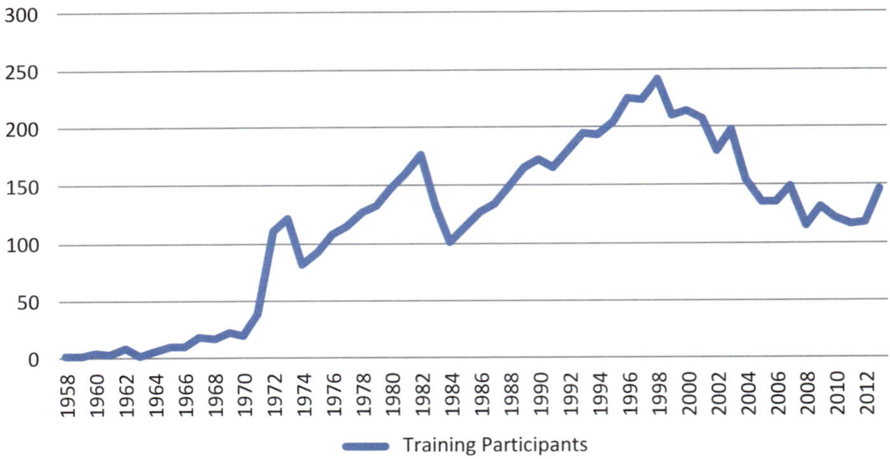

Fig. 6.1 JICA Training Participants from Mexico 1958–2013 (Source: Author's calculations based on data from JICA 2016)

natural resources and energy, disaster management, transportation, among others (JICA 2016). According to Mikami and Furukawa (2014), since 2012 JICA has shifted its assistance goals from impacts at the individual trainee level to impacts at the organizational level, seeking to enable productive environments by employing a qualitative approach.

Historically, Mexico ranks in the top 10 countries of JICA's training assistance beneficiaries with a total of 5841 trainees. As shown in Fig. 6.1, between 1970 and 2012 training participants from Mexico have oscillated between 100 and 250 trainees per year. Also, since the implementation of the Mexico-Japan Economic Partnership Agreement (EPA) in 2005, assistance training to Mexico has been registered between 100 and 150 yearly participants (JICA 2016). It is important to point out that the EPA establishes Japan's Country Assistance Program for Mexico and sets "industry promotion" as its priority area for operation. Within Mexico's assistance plan, the Japanese government formulated a "Program to Strengthen the Competitiveness of SMEs[1] and Supporting Industries" with the overall goals to provide technical support in various elements required for industry promotion and give support to bolster new technology adoption from Mexican SMEs. Under this program, the "Project for Automotive Supply Chain Development in Mexico" (hereafter PASCDM) carried out between 2012 and 2015, stands out as a cooperation project that attempted to strengthen and develop the local supplier base in the automotive industry, expecting improvements that would allow local suppliers to form part of Japanese automotive supplier chains in Mexico.

According to JICA (2015), the PASCDM presented high relevance in terms of priority development policies of Mexico, specific needs of beneficiaries, and Japan's

[1] Small and Medium Size Enterprises.

Official Development Assistance (ODA) policies. Similarly, the Mexican federal government through the national goals set in its National Development Plan 2014–2018 aims to increase competitiveness of micro, small and medium size enterprises and increase their participation in global production chains, especially in strategic industries such as the automotive industry.

The PASCDM selected the states of Queretaro, Guanajuato and Nuevo Leon for implementation, since these states are key locations for the Mexican automotive industry. The state of Nuevo Leon has a developed industrial base with an automotive industry cluster; while Guanajuato has successfully attracted major Japanese Original Equipment Manufacturers (OEMs) that have established car assembly plants. This investment has spurred growth of Japanese auto component suppliers, especially Tier-1 firms in Guanajuato and the neighboring state of Queretaro.

Japan as a major global producer and exporter of automobiles has high technological and know-how levels relevant to the industry and JICA has supported previous projects that promote human resource development and capacity enhancement in the automotive industry in countries such as Thailand and Saudi Arabia. Also, in Mexico, the Japanese government has developed private sector projects including the "Project for Human Resource Development in the Technology of Plastic Transformation" (2010–2014) coordinated by JICA and the "Automotive Industry Sector Development Support Program" (2002–2010) organized by the Japan External Trade Organization (JETRO). Mexican agencies have also promoted the development of local suppliers in the automotive industry. For example, in 2015 the National Auto Parts Industry (INA) and the National Entrepreneurship Institute (INADEM) initiated a program where they would be financing 50% of the costs of the basic quality tools required by Tier-1, Tier-2, and Tier-3 firms interested in becoming suppliers of OEMs. Similarly, Promexico, through its Multinational Accompaniment Model (ACT) seeks to strengthen the local supply chain through business meetings and seminars with the intent of facilitating the incorporation of local Tier-2 and Tier-3 firms as suppliers of OEMs and Tier-1 foreign firms.

Given this background, it becomes relevant to analyze the impact of Japanese training on local firms. Specifically, the present chapter presents an overall outlook of the PASCDM and the results achieved by this project; however, the analysis is focused on the state of Guanajuato, on the technology and knowledge adoption and productivity enhancements achieved by Mexican Tier-2 firms that participated in the TPs during the project. The reason for focusing on the state of Guanajuato is due to the fact that this particular state has been successful in attracting Japanese automotive firms during the last 10 years. The Guanajuato government has set up an overseas office in Tokyo in charge of promoting the state seeking to attract Japanese FDI. Depending on the source, between 62 and 76 Japanese automotive firms are located in Guanajuato and future arrival of more Japanese firms is expected. During the last 7 years, Guanajuato received investment in the automotive sector totaling $7.6 billion USD, which represented nearly 70% of total investment in the state (JICA 2015).

6.2 Literature Review

The positive effects from the transfer of knowledge or technological dissemination in developing countries has been widely analyzed and documented. The focus from the majority of previous literature has been set on Foreign Direct Investment (FDI) as a mechanism to transfer knowledge and enhance the productivity of local firms through different mechanisms with mixed results (Guzman-Anaya 2013). However, TPs offered by assistance plans from developed to developing countries may also serve as channels to transfer technology and knowledge to local firms.

As Mikami and Furukawa (2014) point out, the increase of International Cooperation in the form of Official Development Assistance (ODA), TPs and technical cooperation projects not only from Japan but also from other emerging donors such as China and India has augmented interest on aid effectiveness. For example, the Organisation for Economic Cooperation and Development (OECD) in 2008 recognized within the Accra Agenda for Action on Aid Effectiveness the importance of better coordination and accountability between receiving and donor countries.

According to Mikami and Furukawa (2014) research on training has adopted an inter-disciplinary approach with special interest from labor economics, business administration and development studies. Within the research branch pertaining to labor economics, the main approach has studied the interactions between firms and employees with regards to costs of general training. Through training, employees invest in their human capital stock and increase their productivity. The offering of general training generates a conflict of interests between employees that received training and have an incentive to leave the firm that paid for their instruction, and the company that seeks to recover the benefits from trained workers. Also, employee training creates tensions among competing firms since trained workers can be seen as a common good for all companies creating incentives for free-riding. In conclusion, studies from labor economics have focused on finding optimal levels and equilibrium scenarios for training (Acemoglu 1997; Acemoglu and Pischke 1998; Boom 2005).

Development studies seem to focus on donor-lending training in developing countries and the efficiency and effectiveness of this training. For example, exploring the development of high-level technical and managerial skills in training in the public sector and the brain drain problem of locally and internationally trained civil servants. In this sense, Tessema et al. (2012) conduct a study in Eritrea and find that there is an increasing trend in external brain drain where the best trained and educated young men and women leave for more developed societies. Similarly, the paper shows an increase in internal brain drain, meaning that once civil servants obtain better qualifications from training, they seek employment in the private sector. Another key finding shows that trained human resources being retained seem to be used inefficiently, or in other words not in the positions where they might have a larger economic or social impact.

Studies from the business administration perspective have focused on the outcomes from training at the organizational level; for example, in terms of firm performance and innovation (Bartel 1994; Huang 2001; Almeida and Carneiro

2009; Dumas and Hanchane 2010; Chen et al. 2013). Dearden et al. (2006) and Konings and Vanormelingen (2015) research the relationship between training and wages and training and productivity. Their findings show that training is associated with significant higher levels of productivity and higher wages. Another characteristic of this branch of research is that special interest has been centered on the conditions under which training becomes more effective, in terms of external or internal factors (Nikandrou et al. 2008). Mikami and Furukawa (2014) mention three factors that the literature has proven to matter in training effectiveness: trainee characteristics, training design and work environment.

Mikami and Furukawa (2014) mention two main reasons why there have been longstanding criticisms on the effectiveness of TPs. First, there are doubts whether participants in TPs really learn anything from the courses, especially if there is lack of clear training policies or training participant selection procedures. Second, even if participants learn something there is a tendency for them to leave their organizations after the training, seeking higher wages and better working conditions resulting in internal and external brain drain.

Several empirical studies have analyzed the effectiveness of JICA's TPs. Nakano et al. (2015) investigated the impact of JICA training on the adoption of new rice cultivation technologies and on the productivity in an irrigation scheme in Tanzania. The results showed that through social networks and observation, non-trained farmers learned and adopted the new technologies from trained farmers. The overall result of JICA's training on productivity resulted in an increase from 3.1 tons per hectare in 2008 to 4.7 tons per hectare in 2012 for trained workers, while non-trained farmers increased their productivity from 2.6 tons per hectare in 2008 to 3.7 tons per hectare in 2012. Similarly, Mikami and Furukawa (2014) found that bilateral communication between trainees and their dispatch organization plays a key role in increasing the probability of successful organization-level transfer of individual-level learning, irrespective of the absorptive capacity of the organization. The study also reports the successful case of the National Statistics Office of the Philippines, where 10% of its 3000 employees are former participants of JICA's TPs. The training of staff members from the statistical office has led to the development of capacities needed to replicate and implement their own TPs on statistics to other countries such as Myanmar, Cambodia, Laos, among others.

6.3 Background

According to statistics from the Mexican Automotive Industry Association (AMIA), total automobile production in Mexico reached 3′219,786 units in 2014, amount that ranked the country in the 7th global position regarding automotive vehicle manufacturing. By 2015, total production was registered at 3′367,887 units, representing an increase of 4.6% compared with 2014. Figure 6.2 presents the monthly production figures for 2014, 2015 and part of 2016. Future growth in production of

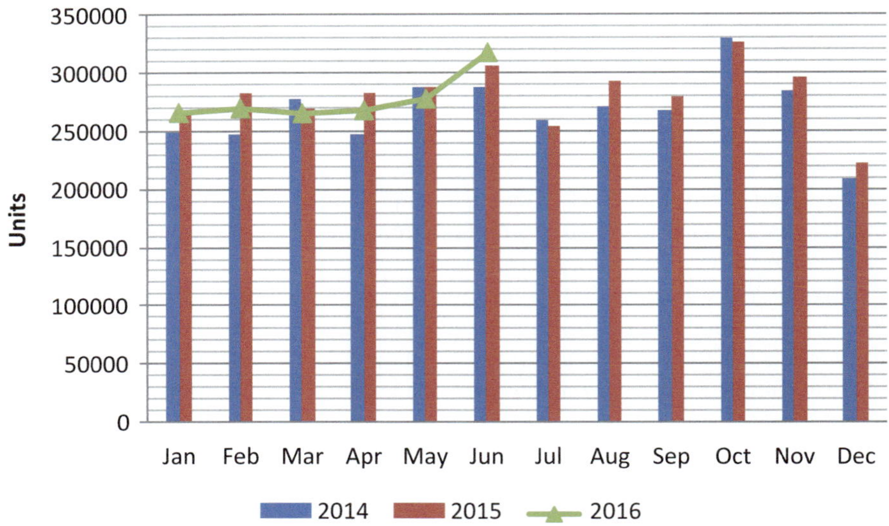

Fig. 6.2 Total Automobile Production in Mexico 2014–2016 (Source: Author's calculations based on data from AMIA 2016)

automobiles is expected for Mexico, primarily due to the construction projects of new plants from Audi, BMW, JV of Daimler/Nissan, Kia and Toyota.

Analyzing the nationality of the automaker, Japanese firms have increased their share in total automobile manufacturing. For example, during the month of February 2016 Japanese production represented almost 44% of total manufactured automobiles, compared with 37% back in February 2015 (AMIA 2016). This is a reflection of an increased interest from Japanese automakers to increase their presence in Mexico as a production hub for the internal and external markets.

Mexican automotive sector exports have also registered an important growth, especially in the North American market, which traditionally has been the main target. During 2015, 87% of total automotive exports were aimed for North America, followed by 4.2% to South America and 3.9% to Europe. Japanese firms in particular, represent 40% of total exports in the industry with a share of 35% of total exports to North America, 64% in South America and 60% in Europe. Also, between 2014 and 2015 Japanese firms exports have increased by 24.5%.

The previous statistics show an increased interest of Japanese firms presence in Mexico's automotive industry and reflect a major dynamism of Japanese Foreign Direct Investment (JFDI) flows to Mexico. With the implementation of the EPA in 2005, the flows of JFDI increased, with a special interest and concentration in the automotive industry. Guzman-Anaya (2013) mentions that during the period from 2003 to 2013, JFDI to Mexico grew at an annual average growth rate of over 20%; additionally, 70% of total investment concentrated in the automotive industry. The sharp increase of automotive JFDI was caused by two main factors: The strategic location of Mexico as a production base for exports to the North American (U.S. and

Canada) and South American market (mainly Brazil), and by an increase in internal demand for automotive products.

However, the increase of JFDI presence in the Mexican automotive industry has highlighted weaknesses in the local supporting industry, especially at the Tier-1 or Tier-2 level. JICA (2015) reports that Mexican companies represent less than 30% of total local auto parts procurement, with clear deficiencies to comply with Japanese firm requirements in terms of quality, costs and delivery times. Similarly, Ramirez-Samano (2016) argues that the low levels of local procurement is due to the lack of information regarding local supplier firms, a knowledge gap from local firms regarding Japanese business practices and production systems. In this sense, Guzman-Anaya (2016) also mentions that quality has been proven to be a determinant factor for presence (or lack of) linkages between Japanese firms and local suppliers. Specifically, the study was carried out in Mexico's western region, and the results showed that local firms that transition from a "bad" perceived level of quality to a "regular" level are six times more likely to be employed as suppliers in Japanese production chains. Another determinant factor reported was length of adjustment of the Japanese firm, providing evidence to the argument that Japanese firms require time to develop relationships in the host country. The results suggest that Japanese firms that have been established in Mexico for 5 years are 1.93 times more likely to employ local suppliers than a newly established firm; after 10 years of establishment the odds ratio increases to 3.74, and after 15 and 20 years the figure increases to 7.22 and 13.97 respectively. Promexico (2016) mentions that the rapidly evolving demand, changing technology and strict quality requirements by OEMs, have created struggles in the supply chain to keep up especially in areas such as raw materials, tool design, production and repair activities, where most of these goods are still imported.

According to JICA (2015), the absence of local suppliers in the automotive industry incentivized the arrival in a first stage of German, Spanish and Japanese Tier-2 firms; however, with the arrival of major Japanese automakers like Mazda and Honda in Guanajuato, a second more rapid stage was observed, with the entry of new Japanese suppliers in the center and western region of Mexico (mainly in the states of Guanajuato, Queretaro, Jalisco and San Luis Potosi).

Also, JICA (2015) using data from the National Industry of Car Parts (INA), reports that in 2010 there were 940 firms in Mexico's automotive industry, with 44% pertaining to Tier-1 firms, 31% to Tier-1/Tier-2 firms, 23% to Tier-2 firms and 2% to Tier-3 firms. Table 6.1 presents the automotive supplier structure in Mexico during 2010. The table shows that most supplier firms are primarily Tier-1 or Tier1/Tier-2 firms, with 60% of total firms concentrated in five states. Also, from the supplier base, 70% of total firms exhibit presence of foreign capital, furthering illustrating the scarcity of local suppliers for the automotive industry.

Despite these facts, Japanese firms have searched for and trained potential Mexican suppliers with success in incorporating several firms in the production process, but still far from being able to adequately satisfy demand with local procurement. JICA (2015) mentions several factors that contribute to this situation, including lack of information, absence of opportunities for business encounters with local suppliers, and to the cultural and business gaps between both countries,

Table 6.1 Automotive supplier structure in Mexico (2010)

Categorization	Tier-1	Tier-1/Tier-2	Tier-2	Tier-3	
	415	287	221	17	
Distribution (main states)	Mexico City	Mexico State	Nuevo Leon	Queretaro	Guanajuato
	168	162	110	102	22
Capital structure[a]	Foreign capital	National capital			
	70%	30%			

Source: JICA (2015)
Notes: The information presented by JICA is based on data from INA
[a]For the capital structure distribution, JETRO included all automotive suppliers in Mexico even those not associated with INA. A total of 1560 companies were included

especially with regards to the unawareness of the Japanese culture in general and of the Japanese production systems in particular. Also, even though state governments have a clear mission to develop the industrial sector of their jurisdiction, they have not answered with agility to the requirements of Japanese firms by promoting new investment or facilitating business encounters between local and Japanese firms.

From the deficiencies mentioned above, emerges a shared interests between the Mexican and Japanese governments to strengthen the productive environment that may allow the development of a supply chain between Japanese suppliers of Tier-1 level (automotive components) and Mexican suppliers of Tier-2 level (automotive parts). The Mexican government requested technical cooperation to the Japanese government via JICA for the establishment of the PASCDM, with participation of the state governments of Guanajuato, Nuevo Leon and Queretaro and the federal government promotion agency ProMexico.

6.4 The Project for Automotive Supply Chain Development in Mexico (PASCDM)

The PASCDM launched for the states of Guanajuato, Queretaro and Nuevo Leon had as its main objective to strengthen and develop the Tier-1 and Tier-2 supply chain in those states. Additionally, it pursued Mexican suppliers of automotive components and parts (Tier-2) to adopt *Kaizen*[2] activities with regards to quality processes, costs and delivery times expecting improvements that would allow them to participate in Japanese automotive supply chains in Mexico. Also, the project expected to enhance Mexican entrepreneurs' understanding concerning *Kaizen,* and

[2]The term "Kaizen" refers to a process of continuous improvement that involves all elements of an organization. It is considered a concept that reflects the best Japanese management practices that helped boost Japanese firms after World War II to world class competitiveness levels during the 1980s. For further information see Imai (1986).

it also looked to expand the impact to government officials regarding Japanese production and business practices.

The project was developed in three phases:

1. Phase 1: November 2012 to March 2014
2. Phase 2: April 2014 to May 2015
3. Phase 3: June 2015 to November 2015

The project had the intention to promote strategic alliances between the state government and local automotive parts suppliers, and also increase support to other key players such as local consultants, technical assistance centers, research centers and universities to develop a network of future assistance to local firms. It is important to point out that the assistance program or what was labeled as the "Master Plan[3]" within the PASCDM was prepared according to the specific needs detected and signaled by state governments searching for the most efficient way to take advantage of the local resources identified in each state. Some of the assistance programs implemented included:

1. *Kaizen* assistance in the production floor
2. Technical and managerial training
3. Commercial encounters
4. Supply of information
5. Financial assistance.

The PASCDM was implemented through the joint efforts and linkages of the following institutions and organizations:

1. Participating institutions:
   (a) Japanese side: JICA
   (b) Mexican side: State governments of Guanajuato, Nuevo Leon, and Queretaro. ProMexico government office.
2. Beneficiaries: Government officials from the participating states and ProMexico, chosen Tier-1 and Tier-2 firms.
3. Joint Coordinating Committee: Formed by JICA's office in Mexico and the Mexican Agency of International Cooperation for Development (AMEXCID). Also, the participating state governments and ProMexico reported on activities implemented during the project. Two annual meetings were held for counseling, assistance and feedback on different topics related with the PASCDM.

The PASCDM invested in the dispatch of Japanese experts to overlook and implement the project. Five experts coordinated the project, and throughout phase 1 and phase 2, a total of 11 experts in each phase provided assistance to participating firms. Also, a total of four courses aimed to increase motivation for *Kaizen* activities

[3] The Master Plan was accompanied by a "Project Design Matrix" (PDM) that was implemented in 2012 and revised on three occasions to its final version in 2015.

Table 6.2 Training courses offered for government officials and tier-2 firms during the PASCDM

Course name	Date	Total government participants	Total Tier-2 participants	Total participants
Management of the strengthening systems for the automotive industry supply chain	August 2013	8	0	8
Training course for Mexican automotive supplier firm managers	March 2014	2	12	14
Training course for Mexican automotive supplier firm entrepreneurs	October 2014	5	12	17
Technical training for Mexican automotive suppliers	June 2015	2	12	14

Source: Author's elaboration using data from JICA (2015)

were held in Japan for both government officials and local Tier-2 firms' directors. The courses offered and participation to each course is presented in Table 6.2.

6.5 Overall Results from the PASCDM

The PASCDM had the main objective of "strengthening the mechanisms for the development of the supply chain between Japanese Tier-1 suppliers and Mexican Tier-2 suppliers in the selected States". Also, there were five expected results for the project:

1. Strengthening of the system for presentation of assistance services for Mexican Tier-2 suppliers.
2. Strengthening of Mexican Tier-2 suppliers to continue *Kaizen* activities related to quality, costs and delivery.
3. Strengthening and development of the Mexican Tier-2 supplier data base.
4. Improve understanding of Japanese commercial practices and *Kaizen* philosophy among Mexican Tier-2 suppliers and state government officials.
5. Increase business opportunities between Japanese Tier-1 suppliers and Mexican Tier-2 suppliers.

The project objective and each expected result were assigned specific indicators to measure accomplishment of each target and afterwards attainment levels were reported. The project objective with its respective indicators and overall results from the PASCDM are presented in Table 6.3.

JICA (2015) mentions that overall, the main objective from the PASCDM was accomplished. The report states that there was an increase in business opportunities between Mexican Tier-2 firms and Japanese Tier-1 firms in part due to the increase and expansion of production activities by Japanese firms in the automotive industry,

Table 6.3 Overall objective and results from the PASCDM

Objective	Target	Step/Route/Tool	Assessment/Evaluation
Further substantial involvement of Tier-2 Mexican SMEs in the supply chain system established and enhanced by Japanese FDI in designated States.	Sustainable mechanisms for the development of the supply chain between Japanese Tier-1 and Mexican Tier-2 firms.	1. Increase in the number of transactions between Mexican Tier-2 and Japanese Tier-1 suppliers.	1. Acknowledgement by 80% of Mexican Tier-2 firms of increase in the number of transactions with Japanese Tier-1 firms.
		2. Commitment of state governments as participants in the business meetings between Japanese Tier-1 and Mexican Tier-2 firms.	2. Acknowledgment by 80% of Mexican Tier-2 firms of effective commitment by state governments.
		3. Implement with Tier-2 suppliers *Kaizen* assistance, seminars and business encounters and develop a supplier database (Tier-2 directory).	3. Each state government drafted a "Master Plan for Tier-2 Assistance" for support after the project. The effects of the training, seminars or database must be further evaluated by each state.

Source: Author's elaboration using data from JICA (2015)

which in turn reflected in an increase of purchase orders to Mexican suppliers. The report also points out that even though it is difficult to link *Kaizen* practices to an increase in sales, the project clearly changed the "consciousness on manufacturing" to participating Mexican Tier-2 firms. This was achieved through the project's activities, including visits and orientations by the Kaizen experts, training in Japan observing best practices and theoretical and practical guidance in seminars.

The PASCDM carried out a survey study titled "business state before and after the introduction of *Kaizen* activities". The report mentioned that 80% of participating Tier-2 firms acknowledged that the assistance received from the project helped generate new transactions or increased the number of transactions with Japanese Tier-1 firms. Similarly, the survey reported that 80% of participating Tier-2 firms that received technical assistance mentioned that the inclusion of state governments in the business meetings contributed to the increase in business opportunities with Japanese Tier-1 firms. Before the ending of the PASCDM each state government drafted a "Master Plan for Tier-2 Assistance" that was designed for support after the project. The effects of the database (Tier-2 directory) or seminars must be further evaluated by each state.

Following the project objective, a superior objective was established. The superior objective "strengthening of the Mexican automotive supply chain" drafted in the PASCDM and its evaluation is presented in Table 6.4.

It is important to point out that according to JICA (2015) the superior objective is expected to be attained within 3–5 year time span after completion of the project,

Table 6.4 Results from the superior objective

Superior objective	Target	Step/Route/Tool	Assessment/Evaluation
Strengthening of the Mexican Automotive Supply Chain.	Sustainable mechanisms for the strengthening of the Mexican Tier-2 supply chain.	1. Increase of local automotive parts procurement by Japanese Tier-1 suppliers.	1. Individual interviews show evidence of increase in local procurement; however there is not enough data to capture tendencies.
		2. Increase accessibility to Mexican Tier-2 firms of assistance services established in the designated states' Master Plans.	2. The states' Master Plans were launched after completion of the PASCDM so there is no data for evaluation. Also, the assistance services plan is still at an early stage of development.

Source: Author's elaboration using data from JICA (2015)

so it is difficult to evaluate the expected results after less than 3 years of conclusion of the PASCDM. The states' Master Plans began after the conclusion of the PASCDM and assistance services are still at early stages of development. Also, the effects from the *Kaizen* training on the participating firms take time to be observed, and the execution of each state's Master Plan is dependent on an appropriate execution and timing with no major changes in State's commercial or industrial policies, especially with regards to the automotive industry.

Despite the lack of sound data for evaluation of the superior objective, there is early evidence from JICA (2015) that positive impacts are observed in terms of an increase in business opportunities and new business ventures between Mexican Tier-2 and Japanese Tier-1 firms. Individual interviews to local firms suggest more business procurement from their Japanese counterparts. Future expansion of Japanese automotive firm presence in Mexico is expected to increase these business opportunities and also augment competition among local suppliers where private industrial organization and state governments must provide the right environments to increase local procurement in the industry.

The first expected result from the PASCDM, "strengthening of the system for presentation of assistance services for Mexican Tier-2 suppliers" and its evaluation is presented in Table 6.5.

A Master Plan for assistance services to Mexican Tier-2 supplies was elaborated for each designated state. The state Master Plan was presented at the fourth session of the Joint Coordination Committee (JCC) held on March 2015. A revision was executed by each state and the final version of the Master Plan was presented at the fifth session of the JCC on September 2015. Also, an Action Plan (annual operations plan) was elaborated to execute and launch the Master Plan. The state Action Plan was presented at the fourth session of the JCC held on March 2015. A revision was performed by each state and the final version of the Action Plan was presented at the fifth session of the JCC on September 2015.

Table 6.5 Results from the expected result #1

Expected result #1	Step/Route/Tool	Assessment/Evaluation
Strengthening of the System for Presentation of Assistance Services for Mexican Tier-2 Suppliers.	1. Elaboration of a Master Plan for assistance services to Mexican Tier-2 suppliers for designated states.	1. A first draft of the Master Plan was presented on March 2015 and a revised version on September 2015.
	2. Create and execute an Action Plan (annual operations plan) to implement the Master Plan.	2. The state Action Plan was presented on March 2015 and the revised version on September 2015.

Source: Author's elaboration using data from JICA (2015)

Table 6.6 Results from the expected result #2

Expected result #2	Step/Route/Tool	Assessment/Evaluation
Strengthening of Mexican Tier-2 Suppliers to Continue *Kaizen* Activities Related to Quality, Costs and Delivery	1. Implement *Kaizen* assistance to local Tier-2 firms and set individual goals in terms of quality, costs and delivery (QCD).	1. After evaluation, over 75% of participating firms that received *Kaizen* training reached their QCD goals.

Source: Author's elaboration using data from JICA (2015)

JICA (2015) mentioned that each state had the faculty to revise their Master Plan and Action Plan according to their individual needs. In certain cases there was a suspension of certain services after a cost analysis. Also in the states of Queretaro and Nuevo Leon there was a series of setbacks due to the change in government officials and operational personnel associated with the project. However, even in those cases the new state government officials received the Master Plan and Action plan to execute them in a timely fashion after the transition.

Table 6.6 presents expected result #2 "Strengthening of Mexican Tier-2 suppliers to continue *Kaizen* activities related to quality, costs and delivery".

According to JICA (2015), in phase 1 a total of 15 Mexican Tier-2 suppliers participated in the project. It was expected that at least 65% of local Tier-2 suppliers that received *Kaizen* assistance reached their goals in terms of quality, costs and delivery (QCD). From an impact study a total of 11 firms reached their goals in terms of QCD. During phase 2, a total of 23 firms participated (including those that continued from phase 1) and 18 reached their QCD goals. From the remaining five firms that did not reach the QCD targets, at least two increased their QCD levels and showed a *Kaizen* improvement.

Another positive impact from the PASCDM is shown by the willingness to continue to implement *Kaizen* philosophy in firms that participated in phase 1, and an overall change in manufacturing mentality for the firms that concluded phase 2. Also, there was a creation of "*Kaizen* groups" in each state as an initiative coming from participating Tier-2 firms to continue support after the conclusion of the project (JICA 2015).

Table 6.7 presents expected result #3 "Strengthening of the Mexican Tier-2 supplier database".

Table 6.7 Results from the expected result #3

Expected result #3	Step/Route/Tool	Assessment/Evaluation
Strengthening of Mexican Tier-2 Supplier Database.	1. Improve the local supplier database to Japanese Tier-1 firms' requirements.	1. At the time of completion of the PASCDM little feedback was received from users, however it seems that further improvement of the interface and data capabilities is required.
	2. Increase the consultation of the supplier database from Japanese Tier-1 firms.	2. The goal was set at 75% of total Tier-1 Japanese firms, however this was not achieved.
	3. Implement a database management system for designated states.	3. A database workgroup was established and Promexico was appointed as the manager of the database

Source: Author's elaboration using data from JICA (2015)

It is important to point out that according to JICA (2015), the three state governments and ProMexico before the PASCDM managed their own supplier databases with difficulties in sharing information across state lines due to confidentiality issues. Also, Japanese suppliers seldom recurred to the state databases and in some cases did not know of its existence. In this sense, Kakihara and Guzman-Anaya (2014) mention for a study carried out in Guanajuato, that Japanese firms used federal, state or local governments as a source for investment or supplier information in only 5% of total cases.

JICA (2015) argues that JETRO developed a database that served as one of the main sources of business information for Japanese investors. The PASCDM set forward a plan to improve the supplier database for the state governments and ProMexico according to the requirements of Japanese Tier-1 suppliers. The final automotive supplier database was compiled and made operational by the three state governments, ProMexico and JETRO and launched on July 2015. The database included a total of 902 Mexican supplier firms, where 43% of firm data came from ProMexico, 26% from JETRO and the rest from participating state governments.

It was expected that 75% of Japanese Tier-1 suppliers would consult the supplier database to search for business ventures. However, this goal was not achieved due to the fact that the indicator was set at an intermediate project evaluation phase.

Finally, for each participating state, there would be a database management system for upkeep of the data. In this sense, the PASCDM established a database workgroup and ProMexico, as manager of the database, determined the operation rules and future plan of activities. At the time of completion of the PASCDM, little feedback from users had been received due to the short time of operation of the database; however, early responses from Japanese suppliers suggest further improvement of the interface and an increase in data capabilities.

Table 6.8 presents expected result #4 "Improve understanding of Japanese commercial practices and *Kaizen* among Mexican Tier-2 suppliers and state government officials".

Table 6.8 Results from the expected result #4

Expected result #4	Step/Route/Tool	Assessment/Evaluation
Improve Understanding of Japanese Commercial Practices and *Kaizen* Philosophy Among Mexican Tier-2 Suppliers and State Government Officials.	1. Administer seminars to transfer knowledge regarding Japanese business practices and *Kaizen* philosophy.	1. After completion of the PASCDM, over 80% of participating Tier-2 firms improved their understanding of Japanese business practices and *Kaizen* philosophy.
	2. Implement Japanese *Kaizen* philosophy in participating Tier-2 firms.	2. Participating Tier-2 firms from the designated states implemented *Kaizen* philosophy in their production processes.
	3. Provide state government officials with specific knowledge and necessary tools to promote business encounters between local and foreign firms within the automotive industry.	3. After receiving training in Japan, government officials showed deeper understanding on supply chain promotion.

Source: Author's elaboration using data from JICA (2015)

The PASCDM expected that after participation in seminars, at least 70% of Tier-2 local firms would better understand Japanese business practices and *Kaizen* philosophy. However, a "Project Impact Survey" carried out by JICA showed that over 80% of Tier-2 firms that received technical assistance improved their understanding of Japanese business practices and *Kaizen.*

Similarly, the PASCDM contemplated that Tier-2 participating firms would put into action Japanese *Kaizen* activities within their production processes. The results showed that all participating firms from the three States implemented *Kaizen* activities in their production lines.

Also, government officials would receive training to provide them with specific knowledge and necessary tools to promote business encounters in the automotive supply chain. After government official training in Japan, surveys showed that there was a deeper understanding regarding the promotion of the automotive supply chain in Mexico.

Overall, the PASCDM showed an impact on the *Kaizen* understanding and a deeper knowledge on Japanese business practices from entrepreneurs, management personnel of Mexican Tier-2 firms and government officials. This was achieved through seminars and theoretical and practical training in Mexico and Japan (JICA 2015).

From the "Project Impact Survey" carried out by JICA, all participating states increased their *Kaizen* practices in terms of firm participation in *Kaizen* activities and in government officials' scores in *Kaizen* related tests.

Table 6.9 presents expected result #5 "Increase business opportunities between Japanese Tier-1 suppliers and Mexican Tier-2 suppliers".

JICA (2015) mentions that the early business meetings organized by state governments observed low participation of Japanese firms due to a lack of event

Table 6.9 Results from the expected result #5

Expected result #5	Step/Route/Tool	Assessment/Evaluation
Increase the number of transactions between Japanese Tier-1 and Mexican Tier-2 Firms.	1. Designated states should organize at least one business meeting between Japanese and Mexican firms.	1. The three designated states organized business meetings at least once a year in their regions.
	2. ProMexico will organize throughout Mexico seminars to transmit the project's activities and best practices	2. ProMexico organized a seminar to present results from the PASCDM only in Guanajuato state.

Source: Author's elaboration using data from JICA (2015)

promotion. However, subsequent events observed higher participation of Japanese firms. Between 2013 and 2015 a total of 12 business encounters were organized; Queretaro organized two in 2013, one in 2014 and two in 2015; Guanajuato organized one for each year of the project and Nuevo Leon organized two in 2013 and one in 2014 and 2015 respectively.

Promexico organized a session to present the results of the PASCDM in the state of Guanajuato. The other two states were not able to celebrate similar sessions due to the change in government officials at the time of completion of the project.

6.6 Results from the PASCDM for the Case of Guanajuato

For a case of analysis, this research focuses on the firms that participated in the PASCDM from the state of Guanajuato using data from JICA (2015). Particularly, the analysis is centered on the *Kaizen* training implemented during the PASCDM and its effects on the productivity of local Tier-2 automotive firms. The main reason for choosing the state of Guanajuato is because of the growing importance of this location for Japanese automotive firms. For example, the Toyo Keizai (2014/2015) directories report a total of 76 automotive firms in Guanajuato, and according to JICA (2015), the Guanajuato government confirms 72 Japanese firms with a total investment of $3745 million USD. Also, during the last 7 years Guanajuato has received 135 investments in the auto and auto parts sector that total $7.6 billion USD, representing 69% of total investment in the state.

The *Kaizen* training in Guanajuato consisted in several activities including theoretical training and practical training. For example, in 2013, six different theoretical training sessions were held with topics related to *Kaizen* philosophy, and four sessions in 2014. All participating tier-2 firms were given practical training in Kaizen activities from Japanese experts at the company location.

At the state level, the Guanajuato government identified potential participant Tier-2 firms for the project and through site visits elaborated an integral diagnostic to define opportunity areas for each firm and set a plan of action. The state govern-

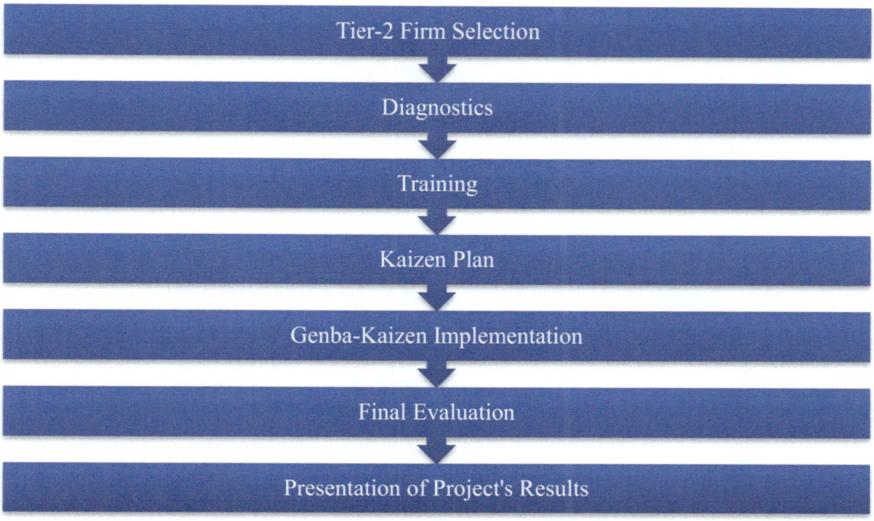

Fig. 6.3 Flow diagram of PASCDM for Guanajuato State (Source: Author's elaboration using data from JICA 2015)

ment in collaboration with JICA offered technical assistance in *Genba-Kaizen*[4] and formed part of the *Kaizen* committee that also included participating firms. Overall training included theoretical courses to operating personnel in specific assistance topics and general training to management and executive levels. Specific courses included training in production floor techniques for plastic injection firms, seminars on Japanese culture and quality control tools management. The flow diagram and action plan for the PASCDM in Guanajuato is presented in Fig. 6.3 and Fig. 6.4 respectively.

Also, for the state of Guanajuato further theoretical and practical training was done through the "State Training Institute" (IECA[5]) for firms specialized in plastic injection molding. The training was conducted with the oversight of JICA's experts at one of the participating Tier-2 firm's location and included theoretical and practical training in topics related with *Kaizen*. According to JICA (2015), the IECA overlooked the training of six participating Tier-2 firms and from their reports, all firms experienced an increase in productivity and in some cases some firms were able to develop new business ventures.

[4]The term "Genba-Kaizen" or what is generally referred as "Gemba-Kaizen" refers to the process of continuous improvement that involves and focuses on the place where the services or products are formed. The "Gemba" is used in Japanese business theory as the place where inputs are transformed into production and where people involved in this space are in the position to suggest improvements to the manufacturing process. For further information see Imai (2012).

[5]The IECA is a public entity that depends from the state government but has legal and budget autonomy to promote training within the state of Guanajuato.

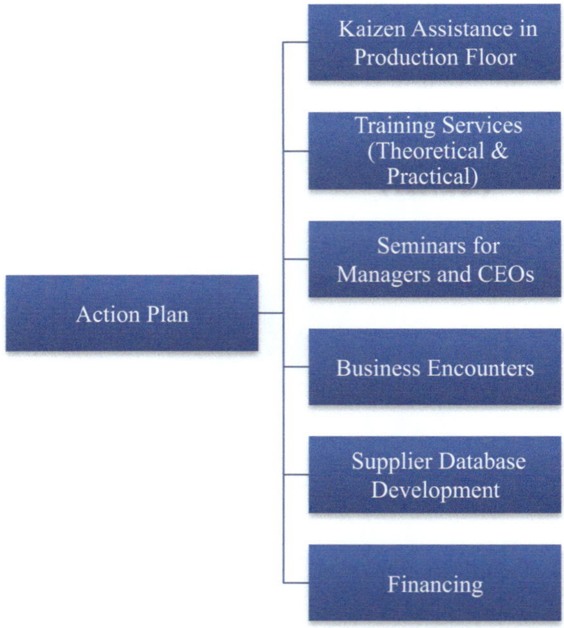

Fig. 6.4 Action plan diagram of PASCDM for Guanajuato State (**Source:** Author's elaboration using data from JICA 2015)

It is important to point out that the IECA was a key player in *Kaizen* support services offered during the PASCDM. The IECA has a network of 28 centers that offer training to Small and Medium Size Enterprises (SMEs). In 2013 they had a total of 1109 trainers, offering 6385 courses to 103,490 beneficiaries with a graduation efficiency of 95.8%. During the project the IECA was part of the process of trainer selection and participated in the visits from Japanese experts to local firms. They also developed courses of their own in topics related with *Kaizen* philosophy (5S, 7 wastes and 3M, Quality Tools, Lean Production Systems, PSC to SQC), and implemented evaluation of the *Kaizen* services through follow up of the technical assistance.

Another key participant during the project was ProMexico, implementing several programs in the three participating states. For the case of Guanajuato, an interesting plan was the "ACT Model", which pursued to increase and strengthen linkages between local and foreign firms through the transfer of Japanese Know-How to Mexican suppliers. Also, ProMexico implemented a survey to identify needs from Japanese Tier-1 firms and conducted business-matching meetings in Japan.

During the PASCDM, a total of 11 Tier-2 firms participated from the state of Guanajuato. Four firms participated during phase 1 of the PASCDM, five different firms during phase 2, and two during both phases. The economic activity of the firms included seven companies specialized in plastic injection molding, two in pressing activities, one in screws and bolts and one in metallic cable manufacturing.

Table 6.10 Phase 1 technical assistance plan and results for Guanajuato State (Six firms)

Technical assistant topic	Firm 1	Firm 2	Firm 3	Firm 4	Firm 5	Firm 6
Strengthening of quality controls	+	+		+		+
Strengthening of process controls	0					
Improve everyday work control through better data collection[a]	0				+	
Reduction of waste following MUDA		+	+	+	0	
Promotion of 5S philosophy[a]		+	+	+	+	+
Strengthening of process control by improving data collection			+			
Optimization of production processes						+

Source: Author's elaboration using data from JICA (2015)
Notes: MUDA is a Japanese concept relating to waste management that is used for optimal allocation of resources
+, –, 0 Indicate an improvement, a worsening or no change in the indicator related to the technical assistance topic respectively
[a]Indicates activities that were voluntary promoted by the firms receiving the training

A first base study to evaluate the *Kaizen* QCD and Japanese Production Control Systems (JPCS) implementation was conducted in June 2013, a first impact study in November 2013, and a second impact study in February 2014. In terms of *Kaizen* QCD, results showed that five out of six firms experienced an increase in their QCD results.[6] Also, in terms of evaluation JPCS, four firms registered an increase in their scores and two did not see any changes between the periods.

A second base study was conducted in October 2014 with its corresponding impact studies in February and May 2015. A total of nine firms were incorporated in the study, where all six firms that participated in the first base study were included. Results showed that in terms of *Kaizen* QCD, all participating firms saw an improvement in their scores; while for the case of JPCS seven improved their overall grade after the second impact study. These findings show that Mexican Tier-2 firms that participated in the PASCDM improved their understanding of the JPCS and their overall levels of quality, costs and delivery times after the training.

In terms of technical assistance, two phases and reports were performed. In phase 1 a total of six firms received technical assistance and a summary of the content and results for each firm are presented in Table 6.10. A more detailed description of the results obtained is presented in the Appendix.

Results from phase 1 show significant improvement in all six firms. Four firms expected to reduce their waste following the MUDA philosophy.[7] From this training,

[6]The comparison is between the base study and impact study #2. The scores were based on the criteria set by the "National Committee on Productivity and Technological Innovation" (COMPITE). The scores are based on a scale that ranges from 1 to 5 where five represents the highest score. For further information see: http://www.compite.org.mx/

[7]MUDA is a Japanese word that translates to "futility, uselessness, wastefulness" that searches for the optimal allocation of resources by eliminating waste. The concept is a key part of the "Toyota Production System" and Lean Management approach to manufacturing.

three firms successfully shortened the time needed to change materials or tools required for production. These benefits directly impact the productivity of these suppliers since they can respond more efficiently to changes in demand for inputs, both in quantity and style (design and materials used) and overall use their resources in a more efficient manner. Only one firm was not able to reduce time in their processes due to changes in personnel after the training.

Another recurrent training topic was quality, where emphasis was placed on reducing the defective rate in firms. In general, the four firms that received this type of training saw improvements in their quality control management. From the reports and results presented in Table 6.10, it stands out that Firm 1 was able to reduce their defect rate from 7% before training to 1% after training. These results are important achievements for local supplier development, as Tokoro (2006) and Guzman-Anaya (2016) mention, improving quality has been a recurrent barrier for Mexican suppliers in joining Japanese production chains.

Also, improving the data collection in three local firms was achieved through implementing diverse mechanisms, for example by using worksheets that allowed the registry of real quality and production data. The supply of real data improved the decision making of local firms and impacted productivity. For example, Firm 1 achieved the technical assistance target of 90% in their productivity levels.

The promotion of 5S philosophy[8] was also implemented in five firms. Interestingly, Firm 2 and Firm 3 voluntarily requested this type of training, highlighting the commitment by local firms in learning Japanese manufacturing techniques. The results showed that a criterion was developed for implementation and evaluation of 5S activities, giving Mexican firms theoretical and practical tools for 5S operation.

The results from phase 1 indicate important improvements in quality achieved through technological and knowledge transfer. However, despite the understanding from local firms about the importance, effectiveness and need for *Kaizen* mentality, in some cases quantitative results were not observed due to the short time frame since the implementation. Also, from the reports of phase 1, it is clear that Mexican suppliers understood and valued the importance of *Kaizen* philosophy and continuous improvement, however it is important to point out that the technological gap of local firms was a barrier that hindered a quicker and deeper implementation of the Japanese manufacturing processes. It is advisable to improve the technological stock of suppliers, at least in terms of technical know-how to better absorb Japanese technology and facilitate technological, knowledge and productivity spillovers.

Also, the fact that the recipients of the *Kaizen* training were all small firms, made the process difficult to implement since only a few employees acquired the knowledge and in some cases more than half of the trainees left the firm. It is important for trainee firms to incorporate the knowledge received by trainees, especially in terms of the *Kaizen* process to allow the flow of information and the implementation of related activities despite high employee rotation.

[8] 5S is a workplace organization method that intends to boost productivity.

Table 6.11 Phase 2 technical assistance plan and results for Guanajuato State (Nine firms)

Technical assistant topic	Firm 1	Firm 2	Firm 3	Firm 4	Firm 5	Firm 6	Firm 7	Firm 8	Firm 9
Strengthening of quality controls	–	+	+	+		–		+	–
Strengthening of process controls	–		+						
Improve everyday work control through better data collection					–				
Reduction of waste following MUDA									
Promotion of 5S philosophy				–		–			
Reduce downtime		+					+	+	
Reduce time needed for production processes	0	+		–	–	–	+	+	+
Improve workflow of people, parts and materials					–		+		+

Source: Author's elaboration using data from JICA (2015)

Notes: MUDA is a Japanese concept relating to waste management that is used for optimal allocation of resources

+, –, 0 Indicate an improvement, a worsening or no change in the indicator related to the technical assistance topic respectively

Phase 2 was implemented between 2014 and 2015 with the participation of nine firms. It is important to point out that the six firms that participated during phase 1 were also incorporated in phase 2. A summary of the results are presented in Table 6.11. Similarly to what was presented for phase 1, a more detailed explanation of the activities for each firm is presented in the Appendix.

During phase 2, emphasis continued on quality improvements and waste reduction. For example firm 2 reported quantitative improvements in the company's quality control systems. The firm understood the importance of quality as a process where all departments need to be involved and initiated interdepartmental meetings to promote the sharing of information. This helped to detect the products with the highest defect rates and the information was used to identify and eliminate the root cause of the problems. The firm also implemented client participation feedback to improve quality criteria and reach quality agreements. Other firms that improved their quality by lowering the defective rates were Firm 4 and Firm 8. On the other hand, Firm 1 and Firm 9 worsen their defective rates after phase 2. For example, Firm 1 had a defect rate of 7% before phase 1 and reached 1% after the completion of the training in 2014, but experienced an increase of the defect rate to 2% after completion of phase 2 in 2015. Similar results were observed for firm 6.

For the case of waste reduction, training sought to reduce downtime or time needed to change tools, materials or standardize procedures. In this sense, not all results from phase 2 were improvements. Several firms that participated in phase 1 experienced time increases after phase 2. Specifically, Firm 1 had a goal to standardize operations to 30 min; in January 2013 the time recorded was at 40 min with no improvement shown by May 2015. Firm 4 reduced time needed to change materials from 45 min to 30 min during phase 1 and saw an increase to 35 min after phase 2. Similar results were reported for firms 5 and 6 with increments in the time needed to change materials from phase 1 to phase 2. From the six participating firms from phase 1 that continued to phase 2, only firm 2 saw an improvement in terms of time reduction after phase 2 and reached the technical assistance objective. The remaining three firms that only participated in phase 2, all saw better time management in different processes.

From these results, it seems that firms that participated in phase 1 of the PASCDM and continued to phase 2 experienced a worsening in some indicators of quality and waste management. Several reasons might explain these phenomena. First, the firms that received the training are all small size companies that although improved during phase 1, may have faced changing market conditions and fail to adapt following their newly acquired training. Also they exhibit low levels of technology, absorptive capacity and high employee turnover that impact the knowledge diffusion of *Kaizen* philosophy. Despite the before mentioned shortcomings, it is clear that overall the PASCDM has successfully transferred knowledge and impacted the productivity of participating firms.

6.7 Conclusions

TPs offered as ODA projects, have traditionally served as mechanisms to transfer technology and knowledge from developed to developing countries. These programs seek to enhance labor force abilities and impact the productivity of local firms. Recently, the increase of International Cooperation in the form of TPs and technical cooperation projects has sparked interest on aid effectiveness. Previous literature has analyzed the effects from TPs from an inter-disciplinary approach. In terms of labor economics, the focus has been set in terms of costs from training and the conflict of interests that arises between employees that benefit from training and employers whom pay for their instruction. Development studies have focused on the efficiency and effectiveness of donor-lending training in developing countries. The business administration perspective has been interested on the organizational level outcomes from training programs, in terms of firm performance and innovation and under which conditions (internal or external factors) training is more effective. Also, several studies have particularly analyzed the effectiveness of JICA's TPs and results show positive effects on productivity and knowledge transfer of trainees in areas such as farming and government sectors in developing countries.

The present study attempted to provide further evidence of the benefits from JICA's TPs analyzing the case of PASCDM implemented in Mexico, following the business administration perspective and focusing on the organizational benefits in terms of productivity achieved through the technological and knowledge transfer administered through various project.

Since early 1950s, JICA has offered TP assistance to over 300,000 participants in nearly 200 countries. Mexico has been one of the benefited countries, and since the implementation of the EPA in 2005 special interest was set on industry promotion and increasing the competitiveness of local SMEs in key supporting industries such as the automotive industry. The reason for promoting development of the supporting automotive industry has been due to the fact that JFDI presence in this industry has spurred since the EPA and this growth has been more accentuated during the last 5 years; it has been estimated that 70% of total JFDI in Mexico is concentrated in the automotive industry.

The sharp increase of automotive JFDI was caused by two main factors: The strategic location of Mexico as a production base for exports to the North American (primarily U.S. and Canada) and South American market (mainly Brazil), and by an increase in demand for automotive products from the internal market. The arrival of Japanese automotive firms sparked interest from the Japanese and Mexican governments to launch the PASCDM as a cooperation project that sought to enhance productivity of Mexican SMEs suppliers. Under this premise the PASCDM was launched to strengthen the mechanisms for the development of the local supporting industry and increase linkages between Japanese Tier-1 suppliers and Mexican Tier-2 suppliers in the participating states.

The aim of this study was to present overall results from the PASCDM and focus on outcomes observed from participating firms in the state of Guanajuato. The reasons for choosing the PASCDM and the state of Guanajuato as case studies were twofold. First, the PASCDM implemented, through joint efforts between Japanese and Mexican development agencies, different TPs aimed to increase understanding of *Kaizen* philosophy and Japanese business practices in local Tier-2 firms and government officials.

Second, the state of Guanajuato has successfully implemented public policies to attract JFDI in the automotive industry. According to Guzman-Anaya (2017), Guanajuato is the second state with major concentration of Japanese firms in Mexico, accounting for 17% of total firms. Guanajuato has successfully attracted Japanese OEMs like Mazda and Honda whom have established car assembly plants in the state and this presence has incited further investment of Japanese auto component suppliers, especially Tier-1 firms. The Toyo Keizai (2014/2015) directories and the Guanajuato State government report between 62 and 76 automotive firms with a total investment of $3475 million USD. Also, during the last 7 years Japanese investment accounts for almost 70% of total investment in the state.

The PASCDM was implemented during 2012 to 2015 in three phases in the states of Guanajuato, Queretaro and Nuevo Leon. The main objective was to strengthen and develop the Tier-1 and Tier-2 automotive supply chain in those states by adopting *Kaizen* philosophy regarding quality processes, costs and delivery times. Also, the project expected to impact entrepreneurs' and government officials´ understanding of *Kaizen* and Japanese business practices. The PASCDM delivered training courses in Mexico and in Japan and dispatched Japanese experts to the participating firms to overlook the *Kaizen* implementation process. The project also provided commercial encounters, financial assistance and supplied information for the development of a Tier-2 supplier database in the participating states.

The results obtained from the JICA (2015) report regarding the PASCDM show a successful technological and knowledge transfer to local firms. In particular, the diffusion of *Kaizen* philosophy and other lean manufacturing tools such as 5S, MUDA, and root cause analysis, directly impacted on the productivity of participating firms by achieving a more efficient use of resources. Focus was placed on continuous improvement, better data collection, interdepartmental flow of information, customer feedback and production programming according to market demand. Also, in some cases processes and production layouts were reorganized to further eliminate waste in firms. These quality and productivity improvements helped the participating firms become more competitive and in several cases propelled them to become suppliers of Japanese Tier-1 firms.

Overall results from the project indicated an increase in business opportunities and sales for Mexican Tier-2 firms with not only Japanese Tier-1 firms but also with other automotive clients. This was achieved in part through improvements in QCD of firms; particularly over 75% of participating firms that received *Kaizen* training reached their goals in QCD. The PASCDM successfully transmitted the *Kaizen* philosophy and provided a deeper knowledge on Japanese business practices to entrepreneurs, management personnel of Mexican Tier-2 firms and government officials through seminars and theoretical and practical training in Mexico and Japan. Finally, the PASCDM achieved the development of a unified supplier database to administer information and facilitate the contact between Japanese Tier-1 and local Tier-2 firms.

For the case of Guanajuato, a total of 11 Tier-2 local firms participated in the PASCDM. Four firms participated during phase 1, five during phase 2, and two during both phases. The economic activity of the firms included seven specialized in plastic injection molding, two in pressing activities, one in screws and bolts and one in metallic cable manufacturing.

As JICA (2015) mentions, it is important to point out that for the state of Guanajuato, the state training institute IECA was a key player in *Kaizen* support services, offering theoretical and practical training during the PASCDM. Particularly, IECA overlooked the training of six participating Tier-2 firms specialized in plastic injection molding and results show that all firms experienced an increase in productivity and in some cases firms were able to develop new business ventures. Similarly, the Mexican government agency ProMexico implemented the "ACT Model", which facilitated the transfer of Japanese Know-How to Mexican suppliers.

Results from phase 1 show significant improvement in all six firms in terms of waste management under the MUDA philosophy. This learning directly impacted the productivity of local firms by allowing them to respond more efficiently to changes in input demand and overall use their resources in a more efficient manner. Also, participating firms saw improvements in their quality control management, which directly impacted on the reduction of their defective rates. Data collection techniques were also provided and permitted the correct and real registry of quality and production data improving the decision making process with further impacts on productivity. Several firms also received theoretical and practical tools for the implementation of 5S philosophy. The results from phase 1 indicate important improvements in productivity and quality, and reflect an effective technological and knowledge transfer to local firms.

Results from phase 2 also reported improvements in quality and waste reduction in most firms, primarily in those that only participated during phase 2 of the PASCDM. Interestingly, the results from the project showed that firms that participated in phase 1 experienced a worsening in some indicators of quality and waste management. This might be explained by the fact that all firms are SMEs characterized by sluggish adaptability to quick changes in market conditions, low levels of absorptive capacities and high employee turnover. Despite the shortcomings, it is clear that all firms are better off than before joining the PASCDM, confirming a successful transfer of knowledge and impact on the productivity of participating firms.

The overall results from the PASCDM and the specific results from the participating firms in Guanajuato show interesting and positive outcomes. Firms improved their QCD and this resulted in better possibilities to supply Japanese firms in the automotive industry. The project also gave firms the groundwork and motivated participants for future improvement of their production processes. For example, there was a creation of "*Kaizen* groups" in each participating state as an initiative of the Tier-2 firms to continue support after the conclusion of the project.

From the results it is clear that participating firms have transitioned towards a Japanese-style production outlook. By visiting Japanese firms and learning about *Kaizen* philosophy, local firms first saw their firm's problems and shortcomings. They learned to value the importance of human resource development to achieve *Kaizen* implementation and manufacturing success. Also, they were taught to search for the root cause of problems within the firm. A participant in phase 1 of the PASCDM mentioned "In Mexico we focus on problems relating to personnel and equipment. Therefore, we tend to solve our problems by downsizing or by buying new machinery. However, after learning about the 5 whys technique, we have learned that our way of thinking was wrong and we have started to search for the root cause of the problems" (JICA 2015, p. A-4-2-9).

Despite the overall success of the PASCDM, several shortcomings were also identified. For example, several firms only applied the *Kaizen* learning to one product line, so horizontal diffusion to other products remained pending. Also, the fact that the recipients of the *Kaizen* training were all small firms hindered the process, since only a few employees acquired the knowledge and in some cases more than half of the trainees left the firm due to high employee rotation. In this sense, it is important for trainee firms to incorporate the knowledge and register the *Kaizen* process to allow the implementation of the activities despite employee rotation. This might be achieved through manuals for the case of explicit knowledge or on the job training and learning-by-doing for the case of tacit knowledge. Also, from the reports of phase 1 it is clear that Mexican suppliers understood and valued the importance of *Kaizen* and continuous improvement, however it is important to point out that the technological gap of local firms was a barrier for a quicker and deeper implementation of the Japanese manufacturing processes. It is advisable to improve the technological stock of suppliers, at least in terms of technical know-how to absorb Japanese technology and facilitate technological, knowledge and productivity spillovers. Finally, even though there was a deeper understanding of Kaizen philosophy by participating Tier-2 firms that directly impacted the QCD levels of these firms, the Japanese Tier-1 suppliers require higher levels of QCD than those agreed and achieved by Mexican firms. This results in an existing difference in perception between QCD requirements among Japanese and Mexican firms that still needs to be reduced.

Also, despite the understanding from local firms about the importance, effectiveness and need for *Kaizen* mentality, in some cases quantitative results were not observed due to the time frame in the implementation. As Nakano et al. (2015) point out, the impact evaluation of training programs should be conducted not in the short-run but at least a few years after implementation, in order to fully capture the spillover effects from training. In this sense, it is advisable to revise the effects of trained firms in the medium term to allow for the newly introduced technologies and knowledge to be fully adopted and the increase in their productivity observable. Future research should revise case studies of participating firms of the PASCDM and revaluate how the project further impacted the productivity of these suppliers.

Japanese interest in developing the local supplier base seems to remain as an important area for cooperation, as was shown by Shinzo Abe's visit to Mexico in July of 2014, where an agreement between both nations was reached to further promote the integration of Mexican SMEs as suppliers of Japanese mid-sized and large companies in Mexico. The topic will thus remain relevant since additional expansion of Japanese automotive firms presence in Mexico is expected and this will bring further business opportunities and increased competition among local suppliers, where cooperation between private industrial organization, educational institutions and state governments will play an important role in providing the right environments to increase local procurement in the industry. In this sense, as Salas (2016) points out, it is also important for the Mexican side to face the challenges accompanied by a rapid industrial growth, where a modernization of the current infrastructure will be vital, especially in terms of improving port capacities, road and railway networks, and logistic processes.

It is also relevant to mention that according to Promexico (2016), over 76% of total input demand in the industry is for imported processes, implying an enormous area of opportunity for foreign and domestic firms in areas such as stamping, smelting, forging and machining. In this sense, Promexico (2016) mentions that the Mexican government is actively pursuing to attract foreign companies that can contribute to the development of the Mexican suppliers with possibilities of technological and knowledge transfer via alliances or joint ventures.

Appendix (Tables 6.12 and 6.13)

Table 6.12 Detailed results from phase 1 for Guanajuato State (Six firms)

Firm	Technical assistance topic	Technical assistance objective	Results phase I 2014
Firm 1	Strengthening of quality controls.	Reduce the defect rate to 3.5%.	The firm had a defect rate of 7% in January 2013 and was reduced to 1% by May 2014.
	Strengthening of process controls.	Establish standardized operations to 30 min.	The firm had operations of 40 min in January 2014 and remained unchanged by May 2014.
	Improve everyday work control through better data collection.[a]	Improve data collection and reach productivity levels of 90%.	Productivity levels were at 90% in January 2013 and remained unchanged by May 2013.
Firm 2	Reduction in waste following MUDA.	Reduce time for changing products and tools to 80 min.	The training provided a better understanding of waste problems in the workplace and tools to identify it.
	Strengthening of quality controls.	Reduce the defective rate to 1000 parts per million (ppm).	The training equipped the firm with a chronological evolution of quality defects.
	Promotion of 5S philosophy.[a]	Reach 50 out of 60 points in 5S evaluation.	A criterion was developed for implementation and evaluation of 5S activities.
Firm 3	Strengthening of process controls by improving data collection.	Reach 20 min of data collection per day.	Mechanisms for data collection were implemented.
	Reduction in waste following MUDA.	Reduce time for changing materials and molds to 15 and 30 min respectively.	Technical assistance was provided for a better shift of materials and molds with noticeable reductions in time.
	Promotion of 5S philosophy.[a]	Reach over 80 points in all areas of the company using the firm's evaluation criterion.	A criterion was developed for evaluation of 5S activities.
Firm 4	Reduction in waste following MUDA.	Reduce time for changing materials to 25 min.	Technical assistance was provided for a better shift of materials and standardization of processes.
	Strengthening of quality controls.	Reduce the defective rate to 100%.	Training in data collection and data analysis in quality cycles was administered.
	Promotion of 5S philosophy.	Reach 100 points.	Training was granted to build an implementation mechanism of continuous improvement for future 5S audit.

(continued)

Table 6.12 (continued)

Firm	Technical assistance topic	Technical assistance objective	Results phase I 2014
Firm 5	Reduction in waste following MUDA.	Reduce time for changing materials to 80 min.	Technical assistance was given but not implemented due to personnel changes.
	Improve the everyday work control trough better data collection.	Improve data collection and reach a defect rate of 0.7%.	Improvements were achieved through creating and using work sheets to collect real quality and production data.
	Promotion of 5S philosophy.	Reach 100 points.	A criterion was developed for implementation and evaluation of 5S activities.
Firm 6	Optimization of production process.	Reduce time for changing materials to 60 min.	Observation and work analysis techniques were used to improve the work and production installations.
	Strengthening of quality controls.	Reduce the defective rate to 0.2%.	Training was administered to better identify the root of problems according to the source (internal or external factors).
	Promotion of 5S philosophy.	Reach 100 points.	Emphasis on baselines of 5S was provided with active employee participation.

Source: Author's elaboration using data from JICA (2015)
Notes: MUDA is a Japanese concept relating to waste management that is used for optimal allocation of resources
[a] Indicates activities that were voluntary promoted by the firms receiving the training
Note: refer the table 6.10

Table 6.13 Detailed results from phase 2 for Guanajuato State (Nine firms)

Firm	Technical assistance topic	Technical assistance objective	Status before phase 2 (2014)	Results after phase 2 (2015)
Firm 1	Reduce the defect rate.	Reach 3.5%.	The defect rate was originally at 7% and after phase 1 was reduced to 1%.	The defect rate increased to 2% after phase 2.
	Establish standardized procedures.	Standardize operations to 30 min.	The time was recorded at 40 min before phase 1 and remained unchanged.	Time reduction was not achieved and remained at 40 min after phase 2.
	Process control.	Maximum of 90%.	Before phase 1 was 90% without change.	The percentage increased to 92%.
Firm 2	Reduction of downtime.	Reduce downtime to 10 min.	Downtime was reported at 30 min.	Downtime was reported at 10 min.
	Quality improvement.	Reach 1500 ppm.	743 ppm (blowing). 94,203 (injection).	The firm reached 860 ppm.
	Reduce time needed to change tools.	Reduce time to 1 hour.	Time noted at 6 hours.	Time noted at 1.3 hours.

(continued)

Table 6.13 (continued)

Firm	Technical assistance topic	Technical assistance objective	Status before phase 2 (2014)	Results after phase 2 (2015)
Firm 3	Intensify the detection of process defects.	Reach 2% of process defects.	The process defect rate was 6.5%.	The process defect rate reached 0.5%.
	Strengthening of controls.	Reach 100%.	Was 40%.	Reached 90%.
Firm 4	Reduce time needed to change materials.	Reduce time to 25 min.	Time was noted at 45 min before phase 1 and was reduced to 30 min.	Time was noted at 35 min after phase 2.
	Reduce the defect rate.	Reach 100%.	Was 70% before phase 1 and remained unchanged.	After phase 2, the firm reached 98.6%
	Implement 5S philosophy.	Reach 100 points.	Firm had 90 points before phase 1 and remained unchanged.	The firm registered 80 points.
Firm 5	Reduce time needed to change materials.	Reduce time to 80 min.	Time was registered at 100 min and was reduced to 95 min after phase 1.	Time was registered at 180 min after phase 2.
	Arrange the workflow of people, parts and materials.	Reach 100 points.	Firm had 91 points before phase 1 and remained unchanged.	Firm registered 80 points after phase 2.
	Acquire correct data.	Reach 0.7%.	Firm noted 8% before phase 1 and 2.8% after phase 1.	Firm reached 2.3% after phase 2.
Firm 6	Reduce time needed to change materials.	Reduce time to 60 min.	Time was registered at 80 min before phase 1 and was reduced to 50 min.	Time was registered at 50 min after phase 2.
	Reduce defects from intern process.	Reach 0.2%	Was 0.6% before phase 1 and was reduced to 0.15%.	Increased to 1.2% after phase 2.
	Implement 5S philosophy.	Reach 100 points.	Firm had 94 points before phase 1 and increased to 95 points.	The firm registered 85 points after phase 2.
Firm 7	Reduce waiting time in forging process.	Reduce waiting time by 50%.	Firm reduced waiting time by 35%.	Firm reduced waiting time by 50%.
	Optimization in tools management.	Reduce by 50%.	Firm reduced to 35%.	Firm reduced to 48%.
	Reduce waiting time in rolling process.	Reduce waiting time by 60%.	Firm reduced waiting time by 10%.	Firm reduced waiting time by 50%.

(continued)

Table 6.13 (continued)

Firm	Technical assistance topic	Technical assistance objective	Status before phase 2 (2014)	Results after phase 2 (2015)
Firm 8	Reduce waiting time in process.	Reduce waiting time to 20 min.	Firm registered waiting time at 147 min.	Firm reduced waiting time to 59 min.
	Reduce the process defect rate.	Reach 4000 ppm.	Was 8138 ppm.	Reached 3464 ppm.
	Reduce stop time due to maintenance.	Reduce stop time by 60%.	Stop time was reduced 10%.	Stop time was reduced 50%.
Firm 9	Reduce time needed to change tools.	Reduce time to 30 min.	Time noted at 80 min.	Time reduced to 60 min.
	Reduce stock.	Reduce time of stock to 5 days for finished and unfinished products.	Stock time was 7 days.	Stock time was reduced to 5 days.
	Reduce defects from intern process.	Reach 2.19%	Was 3.02%.	Increased to 4.11%.

Source: Author's elaboration using data from JICA (2015)
Notes: The six firms that participated in phase 1 also participated in phase 2

References

Acemoglu, D. (1997). Training and innovation in an imperfect labour market. *Review of Economic Studies, 64*(3), 445–464.

Acemoglu, D., & Pischke, J. (1998). Why do firms train? Theory and evidence. *The Quarterly Journal of Economics, 113*(1), 79–119.

Almeida, R., & Carneiro, P. (2009). The returns to firm investments in human capital. *Labour Economics, 16*(1), 97–106.

AMIA. (2016). *Estadísticas Producción Total.* http://www.amia.com.mx/prodtot.html. Accessed 13 July 2016.

Bartel, A. P. (1994). Productivity gains from the implementation of employee training programs. *Industrial Relations, 33*(4), 411–425.

Boom, A. (2005). Firm's investment in general training and the skilled labour market. *Labour Economics, 12*(6), 781–805.

Chen, Y., Hsu, J., & Huang, M. (2013). Lagged effects of training on financial performance: Evidence from longitudinal data. *Global Journal of Business Research, 7*(1), 9–20.

Dearden, L., Reed, H., & Van Reenen, J. (2006). The impact of training on productivity and wages: Evidence from British panel data. *Oxford Bulletin of Economics and Statistics, 68*(4), 397–421.

Dumas, A., & Hanchane, S. (2010). How does job-training increase firm performance? The case of Morocco. *International Journal of Manpower, 31*(5), 585–602.

Guzman-Anaya, L. (2013). *Are productivity spillovers from Japanese FDI larger than U.S. FDI? Inter-industry evidence from Mexico*. Mexico: Universidad de Guadalajara.

Guzman-Anaya, L. (2016). Japanese automotive FDI linkages with local suppliers – Evidence from survey data in Mexico's Western Region. *Green Paper, I.E.S. Seijo University, 72*, 59–72.

Guzman-Anaya, L. (2017). Spatial determinants of Japanese FDI location in Mexico. *México y la Cuenca del Pacífico, 6*(17), 13–35.

Huang, T. C. (2001). The relation of training practices and organizational performance in small and medium size enterprises. *Education + Training, 43*(8/9), 437–444.
Imai, M. (1986). *Kaizen: The key to Japan's competitive success*. New York: McGraw-Hill.
Imai, M. (2012). *Gemba Kaizen: A commonsense approach to a continous improvement strategy*. New York: McGraw-Hill.
JICA. (2015). *Proyecto para el fortalecimiento de la cadena de proveeduría del sector automotriz en México: Informe de terminación del proyecto*. Mexico: Japan International Cooperation Agency (JICA).
JICA. (2016). *JICA activities in Mexico*. http://www.jica.go.jp/mexico/english/activities/. Accessed 05Aug 2016.
Kakihara, T., & Guzman-Anaya, L. (2014). Factores de Localización de la Inversión Extranjera Directa Japonesa en México. In T. Okabe & S. Carrillo (Eds.), *Relaciones México-Japón en el contexto del Acuerdo de Asociación Económica* (pp. 135–173). Mexico: Juan Pablos Editor.
Konings, J., & Vanormelingen, S. (2015). The impact of training on productivity and wages: Firm-level evidence. *The Review of Economics and Statistics, 97*(2), 485–497.
Mikami, S., & Furukawa, M. (2014, November). *An empirical study of the conditions for successful knowledge transfer in training programs* (JICA-RI Working Paper, 85).
Nakano, Y., Tsusaka, T. W., Aida, T., & Pede, V. O. (2015, March). *The impact of training on technology adoption and productivity of rice farming in Tanzania: Is farmer-to-farmer extension effective?* (JICA-RI Working Paper, 90).
Nikandrou, I., Apospori, E., Panayotopoulou, L., Stavrou, E. T., & Papalexandris, N. (2008). Training and firm performance in Europe: The impact of national and organizational characteristics. *The International Journal of Human Resource Management, 19*(11), 2057–2078.
Promexico. (2016). *The Mexican automotive industry: Current situation, challenges and opportunities*. Mexico: Proméxico.
Ramirez-Samano, L. A. (2016). Strengthening the supply chain of the automotive sector in Mexico. *Negocios Promexico,* November–December, 38–41.
Salas, B. (2016). Japanese companies in Mexico set to top 1,000. *Negocios Promexico,* November–December, 10–13.
Tessema, M., Winrow, B., & Teclezion, M. (2012). The transfer of training at macro level in least developing countries: A case study of the "Brain Drain" in Eritrea. *International Journal of Training and Development, 16*(4), 247–262.
Tokoro, Y. (2006). México y Japón: Una Perspectiva del Acuerdo de Asociación Económica. *EconomíaUNAM, 3*(7), 47–68.
Toyo Keizai Inc. (2014). *Kaigai Shinshutsu Kigyou Souran*. Tokyo: Toyo Keizai Inc.
Toyo Keizai Inc. (2015). *Kaigai Shinshutsu Kigyou Souran*. Tokyo: Toyo Keizai Inc.

MIX
Papier aus verantwortungsvollen Quellen
Paper from responsible sources
FSC® C105338

If you have any concerns about our products,
you can contact us on
ProductSafety@springernature.com

In case Publisher is established outside the EU,
the EU authorized representative is:
Springer Nature Customer Service Center GmbH
Europaplatz 3, 69115 Heidelberg, Germany

Printed by Libri Plureos GmbH
in Hamburg, Germany